T0340405

ENRICHING ENGLISH
Curriculum with soul

**A practical guide
for English teams
and leaders**

Jo Heathcote

William Collins' dream of knowledge for all began with the publication of his first book in 1819.

A self-educated mill worker, he not only enriched millions of lives, but also founded a flourishing publishing house. Today, staying true to this spirit, Collins books are packed with inspiration, innovation and practical expertise. They place you at the centre of a world of possibility and give you exactly what you need to explore it.

Collins. Freedom to teach.

Published by Collins
An imprint of HarperCollinsPublishers
The News Building
1 London Bridge Street
London
SE1 9GF
UK

HarperCollinsPublishers
Macken House,
39/40 Mayor Street Upper,
Dublin 1,
D01 C9W8,
Ireland

Browse the complete Collins catalogue at
collinseducation.com

© HarperCollinsPublishers Limited 2023

10 9 8 7 6 5 4 3 2 1

ISBN 978-0-00-864090-3

British Library Cataloguing-in-Publication Data
A catalogue record for this publication is available from the British Library.

At the time of publication, the publishers acknowledge that sites and hyperlinks were verified and bear no responsibility for any subsequent URL domain change.

Author: Jo Heathcote
Publisher: Katie Sergeant
Product Manager: Cathy Martin
Product developer: Saaleh Patel
Development editor: Marian Olney
Copyeditor: Jo Kemp
Proofreader: Catherine Dakin
Cover designer: Amparo Barrera, Kneath Associates
Internal designer and typesetter: 2Hoots Publishing Services Ltd
Production controller: Alhady Ali

Printed and bound in Great Britain by Martins the Printers.

Contents

Chapter 1: Embarking on the Cohesive Journey

What makes a cohesive curriculum in secondary English?

Creating a curriculum for the study of English in a secondary school context is a privilege. It is a brilliant and open-ended opportunity for a passionate practitioner with a deep love of their subject to be able to develop a creative vision for the teaching of English that will impact on the successful education of hundreds, if not thousands, of students.

On a personal level, I find it heartbreaking to hear many fellow practitioners speaking of the narrowness of the English curriculum, of how restrictive it is, how desperately unengaging and how unsuited it is to this demographic of student or that. And I often wonder what might happen if we all, as practitioners, had the time and space to stop and take stock – even for an hour or two – and consider the capacity we have to create an enriching and stimulating curriculum. The opportunity is there, within the subject of English, to educate the whole person and, in my opinion, the work of the English practitioner can be life-changing for the students in our care.

My own experience of English was life-changing indeed, coming as I did from a dingy small mill town in the dreariest end of Yorkshire. My secondary teachers and my Manchester Poly lecturers were collectively brilliant, clever and funny; slightly bonkers in some cases, slightly wild in others. They totally shaped me and not just into a career which paid the bills.

'There is all human life in an English lesson!' declared Vanda, my A-Level English teacher, on more than one occasion in 1985, sweeping her Laura Ashley-clad arm in a dramatic arc and leaving a tantalising cloud of her signature Avon fragrance in the sultry afternoon air. It was always a brilliant and perfectly true reflection of her teaching of Shakespeare, Miller, Heller, Austen, Pope, Hughes and everything else she managed to squeeze in alongside the eight set texts. How on earth did we also manage to read *Hamlet* and *Godot*, Yeats and a million random poems, some of which have stayed with me my whole life?

Vanda was right. There *is* all human life in an English lesson. There is history, there is politics, there is philosophy, there is science, there is psychology, there is sociology. And that's why we, as English practitioners, are dangerous. As a subject, English is a touchstone for political awareness, for emotional intelligence, for critical thinking – all of which are needed more than ever in our increasingly divided, increasingly homogenised, post-truth society. It's also why we are often led to believe the English curriculum is narrow, prescriptive, unengaging and unrepresentative, for how else would we be kept under control?

Task

Begin by downloading and taking a fresh look at the National Curriculum Programmes of Study for English at Key Stage 3 and Key Stage 4, and alongside them download the Programmes of Study for another core subject... let's go with Science.

- What do you notice?
- What seems to be missing from the English Programmes of Study that is there in abundance in the Science documents?

Now, let's take a look together:

Subject content – Biology

Biology is the science of living organisms (including animals, plants, fungi and microorganisms) and their interactions with each other and the environment. The study of biology involves collecting and interpreting information about the natural world to identify patterns and relate possible cause and effect. Biology is used to help humans improve their own lives and to understand the world around them.

Students should be helped to understand how, through the ideas of biology, the complex and diverse phenomena of the natural world can be described in terms of a number of key ideas which are of universal application, and which can be illustrated in the separate topics set out below. These ideas include:

Subject content – Chemistry

Chemistry is the science of the composition, structure, properties and reactions of matter, understood in terms of atoms, atomic particles and the way they are arranged and link together. It is concerned with the synthesis, formulation, analysis and characteristic properties of substances and materials of all kinds.

Students should be helped to appreciate the achievements of chemistry in showing how the complex and diverse phenomena of both the natural and man-made worlds can be described in terms of a number of key ideas which are of universal application, and which can be illustrated in the separate topics set out below. These ideas include:

Subject content – Physics

Physics is the science of the fundamental concepts of field, force, radiation and particle structures, which are inter-linked to form unified models of the behaviour of the material universe. From such models, a wide range of ideas, from the broadest issue of the development of the universe over time to the numerous and detailed ways in which new technologies may be invented, have emerged. These have enriched both our basic understanding of, and our many adaptations to, our material environment.

Students should be helped to understand how, through the ideas of physics, the complex and diverse phenomena of the natural world can be described in terms of a number of key ideas which are of universal application and which can be illustrated in the separate topics set out below. These ideas include:

Each of these paragraphs is followed by pages and pages of subject content: the periodic table, photosynthesis, motion and forces, light waves, atoms, respiration... enough to leave you breathless.

Now take a look at English... erm, well, it seems to suggest we should do some Reading, some Writing, know a bit of Grammar and Vocabulary and do a bit of Speaking in and amongst it all. Where are our pages and pages of subject content? Our topics? At Key Stage 3 someone somewhere was struggling to fill up the template and added a nineteen-page glossary of grammatical terms just to pad it out a bit. At Key Stage 4 they gave up the ghost at page 7.

Where is this narrow and prescriptive curriculum? Our only real parameters occur in Reading. At Key Stage 3 there is a requirement to do a lot of it and ensure we include two Shakespeare plays. Here it is:

Reading

Pupils should be taught to:

- develop an appreciation and love of reading, and read increasingly challenging material independently through:
    - reading a wide range of fiction and non-fiction, including in particular whole books, short stories, poems and plays with a wide coverage of genres, historical periods, forms and authors. The range will include high-quality works from:
        - English literature, both pre-1914 and contemporary, including prose, poetry and drama
        - Shakespeare (two plays)
        - seminal world literature
    - choosing and reading books independently for challenge, interest and enjoyment.
    - re-reading books encountered earlier to increase familiarity with them and provide a basis for making comparisons.

Sounds good to me. And at Key Stage 4?

Reading

Pupils should be taught to:

- read and appreciate the depth and power of the English literary heritage through:
    - reading a wide range of high-quality, challenging, classic literature and extended literary non-fiction, such as essays, reviews and journalism. This writing should include whole texts. The range will include:
        - at least one play by Shakespeare
        - works from the 19th, 20th and 21st centuries
        - poetry since 1789, including representative Romantic poetry
    - re-reading literature and other writing as a basis for making comparisons
    - choosing and reading books independently for challenge, interest and enjoyment.

If we think carefully about these parameters, there is nothing here to tell us as practitioners what we *can't* do. The lack of specified subject content, the lack of specified texts, the lack of prescription throughout is liberating, and gives us the freedom to develop and establish a joyful, cohesive curriculum for all our students, which can be matched and curated to the needs of our particular contexts and settings.

It is often the case, I feel, that we become consumed by the examination syllabus and the demands of this become the 'be all and end all' of our curriculum. In many cases, this relates to English Literature. The pursuit and the coverage of the 'set texts' becomes a chore rather than a pleasure and the grounds (in many cases) for arguments that the curriculum is narrow and unrepresentative. But the curriculum is what we make of it.

Hopefully, within these pages, you will begin to feel a sense of ownership and freedom over your English curriculum as we look for the positives and the opportunities it affords. In creating a cohesive English curriculum, we need to be strategic. The choices we actually have can be overwhelming, and this is often reflected in the varieties of English curricula I have seen at work in many secondary schools.

In some cases, the much-hyped reforms to GCSE, promising depth and challenge and an end to half a million students each year writing about *Of Mice and Men*, meant that some schools heavily weighted their schemes of work towards nineteenth century 'classic' texts. How many of us have bought into the idea that those texts are the only ones of value, when they don't necessarily speak to our students or their experiences at all?

In other cases, I have seen Key Stage 3 curricula so packed with content they are like degree courses and would surely give no 11- or 12-year-old time to develop or embed any of the skills and knowledge they race to pack in. Indeed, some departments have confessed that they struggle to get through all of the schemes of work in the time they have. So, what does that tell us about the schemes of work and the amount of content that has been generated? It would be a good opportunity now to stop and take stock of your own English curriculum and ask yourself a few pertinent questions about its effectiveness and cohesion.

In creating any cohesive curriculum, I would ask all practitioners to think about the secondary English experience as a five-year journey, not as three years followed by two.

Consider the end goal: at the end of five years of study, we want our students to sit their GCSE English examinations in both Language and Literature and achieve individual success. However, we would surely also like to send our students into their futures as confident communicators and critical readers, able to navigate the seemingly infinite amount of information that is thrown at us every day in an increasingly complex world. I, personally, have always wanted my own students to leave my care loving the subject – or at the very least liking it – so that in the future they will still pick up a book, love a good drama, and not say, 'I hate poetry'. So where do we begin?

Begin where the students are at

For most students the transition to secondary school is a big step. They are moving from a potentially small primary school, where even in Year 6 the vast majority of lessons are with one member of staff, into a secondary environment with many different subject teachers. As practitioners of a core subject, we are likely to see students more regularly than, say, a Design Technology teacher. We are welcoming into secondary English a large body of students who have come from several primary schools. What do we know about them and their experiences of our subject?

In some secondary schools, much time is spent doing valuable primary liaison work. I would suggest this is absolutely invaluable to any English team. Admissions information will show you which primary schools your new cohort is coming from. If you have a dedicated primary liaison coordinator in your school, they can be your point of contact with the Year 6 teachers. If not, it can be time well spent to make a summer term call to each school and do a spot of information gathering. If, as in some cases, you have 20–30 feeder schools, this job can be shared between members of the department, each given pre-prepared questions. Even better, what about a joint CPD afternoon to share information? Questions to ask the schools could be:

- What has been covered in Year 6 English?
- What class readers have they used?
- Have these books just been read aloud in class or has significant comprehension and creative work been done on them?
- What different methods have been taught for reading comprehension work?
- Have students had an introduction to Shakespeare?

We have all had the experience of bright-eyed Year 7s cheerfully informing us they have 'done' *Macbeth* when in reality they have read Scene 1, coloured in some witches and created a spell on a worksheet. Aim to get a very clear picture of the range of primary English experiences your new cohort has had, to inform where your starting point will be.

You will have data about your new intake and, in some cases, depending on your school context, this may be used to organise students into sets straight away. This can be problematic in the sense that it doesn't give you a full subject-specific picture of your students. Like any school under examination pressure, primaries focus on preparing students for Key Stage 2 SATs. Is that a true measure of what they can do outside the parameters of that rather challenging examination? SATs exams happen in May. We meet students approximately four months later, after a long summer holiday where many will not have had access to books and may not have picked up a pen.

Your school setting may organise its own diagnostic tests as students enter school in Year 7: Cognitive Abilities Tests (CATs) or similar. These can be very useful but again, only give a partial picture.

At the point you meet new Year 7s – possibly already organised into sets for you – have you seen any of their writing? Have you been able to evaluate their oracy skills? Possibly not. I would always advocate planning in some time at the start of Year 7 to do some diagnostic work which is English specific. Allow perhaps two weeks and include:

- The opportunity to hear everyone read aloud to check for fluency – individually if possible.
- The use of a simple diagnostic reading-age test to ensure you know the reading age of every student. Test again at the end of the year before Year 8. (Bear in mind that the reading age of texts on GCSE English examination papers is approximately 14 years. How far do you need to move students across their five-year journey?)
- The chance for students to work in a team on a task and present back. Who takes the lead? Who is more reticent?
- The chance to construct a piece of creative writing without giving success criteria so you can see if students paragraph or use punctuation without being prompted. What is their level of vocabulary like? What is their spelling like?
- The opportunity to complete a short comprehension task. How do students approach it? Do they use quotations to support their answers? Do they retell or paraphrase?

In this time, watch your students and learn from them. At the end of this observation phase, meet with your team and share findings. If you work in a mixed-ability setting, what additional information have you gathered on the specific kinds of support some students may need? Who is going to need more stretch and challenge exercises? How might you be able to create a seating plan that encourages effective 'buddying'? For example, a student who is orally confident but struggles with spelling will benefit from sitting with a quieter student who has stronger technical skills, and vice versa, when there are opportunities for think/pair/share. In a context where students are in sets from the start, this gives an invaluable subject-specific cross-check against external data and can allow for more precision in setting. More generally, it will ensure that your whole department or team is aware of the needs of each student in their care from very early on in their secondary journey.

So now we can turn our thoughts to planning that journey.

The five-year journey

Let's begin with a clean slate. For many of us, our days in school are already
organised into blocks of time structured around the termly or half-termly breaks.
These help us to organise units of work across the year. While some topics and
texts may need more than these approximately six-week blocks of time, it can be
difficult for students to maintain interest and engagement if units stray too far
beyond this. Take a minute to savour the possibilities and the freedom!

	Autumn 1	Autumn 2	Spring 1	Spring 2	Summer 1	Summer 2
Year 7						
Year 8						
Year 9						
Year 10						
Year 11						

In planning our secondary English curriculum we must, of course, take into
account that the end product of our vision and hard work will realistically be the
examination results of our students. Your chosen examination syllabus in English
Language and English Literature will govern much of what you *choose* to teach
and when in Years 10 and 11. However, when working with departments, I would
always ask them to consider the order in which they teach their GCSE courses and
to reflect on this and evaluate if they are taking the most logical approach.

In many cases, colleagues worry about 'getting through' the Literature
texts, leaving Language work until later in the course, sometimes almost as
an afterthought. In Literature papers, the general requirement across all boards is
to write longer, more critically evaluative essay responses to whole texts. However,
the English Language papers provide more of a scaffolded journey through
shorter-answer questions. In this way they can provide a stepped journey of
skills building in readiness for Literature responses. Take a look at the assessment
objectives for both courses: these are common to all examination boards
and specifications.

English Language		English Literature		
READING (50%) **Read and understand a range of texts to:**		**A01**	Read, understand and respond to texts Students should be able to: • maintain a critical style and develop an informed personal response • use textual references, including quotations, to support and illustrate interpretations.	35-40%
A01	• Identify and interpret explicit and implicit information and ideas • Select and synthesise evidence from different texts			
A02	Explain, comment on and analyse how writers use language and structure to achieve effects and influence readers, using relevant subject terminology to support their views			
A03	Compare writers' ideas and perspectives, as well as how these are conveyed, across two or more texts	**A02**	Analyse the language, form and structure used by a writer to create meanings and effects, using relevant subject terminology where appropriate	40-45%
A04	Evaluate texts critically and support this with appropriate textual references			
WRITING (50%)		**A03**	Show understanding of the relationships between texts and the contexts in which they were written	15-20%
A05	• Communicate clearly, effectively and imaginatively, selecting and adapting tone, style and register for different forms, purposes and audiences • Organise information and ideas, using structural and grammatical features to support coherence and cohesion of texts	**A04**	Use a range of vocabulary and sentence structures for clarity, purpose and effect, with accurate spelling and punctuation	5%
A06	Candidates must use a range of vocabulary and sentence structures for clarity, purpose and effect, with accurate spelling and punctuation. (This requirement must constitute 20% of the marks for each specification as a whole.)	In each specification as a whole, 20-25% of the marks should require candidates to show the abilities described in A01, A02 and A03 through tasks which require them to make comparisons across texts.		

Reflect

• How do the assessment objectives for GCSE English Language differ from those for English Literature?

• How might they provide a more stepped learning journey into the demands of the Literature responses?

• What do they have in common that would help students to make a more scaffolded learning journey?

The idea of the logical and stepped learning journey was one which I reflected on some years ago when I wrote a textbook for English Language at post-16. My aim was to disseminate the GCSE course into a thirty-week programme of study. I had taught in a sixth form college for thirteen years, working with many hundreds of GCSE resit candidates who completed a resit in one academic year. One of my main concerns when examination reform happened was the loss of the Foundation Tier in English examinations for which I had been the Principal Examiner for a major awarding body. This was a particular concern for me in terms of the students who have become labelled 'The Forgotten Third' (ASCL Report 2019), for they were the ones who came to college needing to resit GCSE English Language. Indeed, many of those students had been 'my' candidates on the Foundation Tier and they were certainly never forgotten by me.

As I planned my course and then my textbook, one of the key things I considered was how to use those thirty weeks most effectively so that the key skills and the knowledge needed to answer questions were layered in a logical way. I sequenced the course so that work on comprehension skills, using prose fiction, was followed by narrative writing. Students could then use their experiences of reading and understanding prose fiction to aid their own writing of stories. Subsequently, I went on to explore the analysis of the language and structure of texts in reading before applying that knowledge of the writer's craft to descriptive writing. Only then, when students had embedded skills of comprehension and analysis, did I tackle critical evaluation which pulls those skills together. Here's the contents list from my student textbook, *AQA GCSE English Language for post-16: A one-year course*:

Contents

When I moved back into secondary English teaching, taking over a department in need of a major restructure, I applied the same principles. How could I use the two-year Key Stage 4 course to interleave the skills and knowledge needed to bring about success most effectively in both English GCSEs? This was the starting point for my five-year curriculum rebuild, beginning with my chosen GCSE specifications from which I then worked backwards to Key Stage 3.

The mapping of the GCSE curriculum was designed to interleave the two courses to achieve a balance of time for longer set texts while thoroughly embedding the learning journey through English Language in Year 10, thus helping students build skills and stamina for the longer, more complex essay-type responses required in Literature.

So, we might begin to assemble our five-year plan by adding in those elements first. My own looked like the following example:

	Autumn 1	Autumn 2	Spring 1	Spring 2	Summer 1	Summer 2
Year 10	20th and 21st Century Fiction AQA GCSE English Language Paper 1 Skills and Knowledge Narrative writing	Poetry anthology: Power and Conflict AQA GCSE English Literature Paper 2 Skills and Knowledge Descriptive writing	Drama *An Inspector Calls* AQA GCSE English Literature Paper 2 Skills and Knowledge	19th Century and Modern Non-fiction AQA GCSE English Language Paper 2 Skills and Knowledge	Shakespeare *Macbeth* AQA GCSE English Literature Paper 1 Skills and Knowledge End of Year 10 Assessments Spoken Language Assessment	
Year 11	Unseen Poetry × 4 weeks 19th Century Novel × 8 weeks *A Christmas Carol* AQA GCSE English Literature Papers 1 and 2 Skills and Knowledge Mock examinations		Revision AQA Paper 1 GCSE English Language AQA Paper 2 GCSE English Literature	Revision AQA Paper 2 GCSE English Language AQA Paper 1 GCSE English Literature Final mocks	Revision and start of final exam period Closing the final gaps	Final exam period

Notes: For the AQA GCSE specification in English Language, modern prose fiction is used as the source material on English Language Paper 1 with questions testing AO1 simple retrieval; AO2 analysis of language; AO2 analysis of structure; and AO4 critical evaluation; followed by an AO5/6 creative writing task. Paper 2 contains two items of source material which are non-fiction with questions focusing on AO1 true/false statements; AO1 comprehension; AO2 language analysis; and AO3 comparison. This is followed by a writing task which is more transactional in nature testing AO5/6. Paper 2 contains one source from the nineteenth century.

Reflect

Look over the possible plan for Key Stage 4 on the previous page and make some notes on the following. This could form the basis of a discussion in your department teams.

- How might teaching the knowledge and analytical skills for the shorter-answer language and structure questions in English Language first help to build student knowledge for their work on poetry?

- How might work on poetry enhance student responses to descriptive writing tasks?

- What is the benefit for students of teaching the modern fiction text before Shakespeare or the nineteenth-century novel?

- How might 'stepping back in time' through a text like *An Inspector Calls* help to prepare students for working with nineteenth-century non-fiction? What themes might cross over here that you could link?

- How can you build an overarching theme through Year 10 through your choice of set texts?

- How can you add breadth and diversity through the choices of source material for English Language?

- What is the benefit of teaching Shakespeare over a whole term? Why link this with the Spoken Assessment?

- What opportunities does teaching Unseen Poetry at the start of Year 11 afford you?

- How have students been prepared for the nineteenth-century novel and its assessment?

- What do you notice about the time that is still available for identifying gaps, reteaching, and revision following mock examinations?

Task

Using a grid similar to the one on the previous page and your notes from the reflection exercise, map out a sequence for your Key Stage 4 courses which takes into account the particular specification you follow and the text choices you have made.

- What could improve or enhance the way the course is taught at the moment?
- How could this approach simplify the cognitive load for students?
- How might this approach create more time and space for reteaching and revision?

At this point, I realise you may be asking: 'But, how on earth, in that amount of time, can we get through the texts and teach students how to answer the questions, practise the questions, understand the different tasks on the examination paper for both GCSEs?' The answer lies not in Key Stage 4, but in Key Stage 3.

Creating seamless transition

By suggesting that the answer lies in Key Stage 3, I absolutely do not mean embarking on GCSE content in Years 9, 8 and 7: this is an approach which I personally have never subscribed to, even before Ofsted twigged it was happening and made it a thing. It has always been my strong belief that Year 9 should not became a default position to begin the study of GCSE. Given that many colleagues seemingly feel restricted by GCSE, surely Key Stage 3 is the place to explore, be adventurous and teach outside the box. And those three years are a time to be relished and cherished. Sadly, in many cases, the demise of Key Stage 3 SATs, which colleagues campaigned long and hard for, seems to have opened up chasms in some curricula which have been too handily filled with GCSE texts.

For me, the idea of 'getting some of the poetry done' or reading *Macbeth* in Year 9 feels counterproductive and a wasted opportunity, though I am sure many colleagues may have different views. I have always felt that giving students breadth of experience across Key Stage 3 sets them up more readily for Key Stage 4.

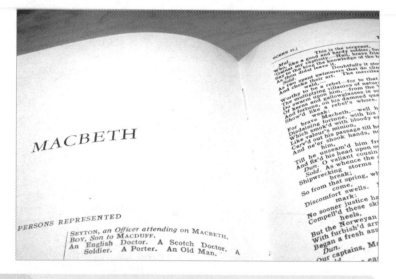

Reflect

Consider how you could use your GCSE half-termly plans as 'anchor points' at the end of a spiral through Key Stage 3. For example, you could:

- teach modern prose fiction with *every* year group in Autumn term 1, leading up to the GCSE prose fiction study in Year 10

- use the summer term to teach a different Shakespeare play in Years 7, 8 and 9, leading up to the GCSE Shakespeare study in Year 10.

Those topic and genre headings have been added to the top of each column of the planning grid. With these logical stepping-stones in place through Key Stage 3, what breadth and range could you now include in your curriculum?

	Autumn 1 Modern prose fiction	Autumn 2 Poetry anthologies	Spring 1 Drama text	Spring 2 19th century project	Summer 1 and 2 Shakespeare text Writing	
Year 10	20th and 21st Century Fiction AQA GCSE English Language Paper 1 Skills and Knowledge Narrative Writing	Poetry anthology: Power and Conflict AQA GCSE English Literature Paper 2 Skills and Knowledge Descriptive Writing	Drama *An Inspector Calls* AQA GCSE English Literature Paper 2 Skills and Knowledge	19th Century and Modern Non-fiction AQA GCSE English Language Paper 2 Skills and Knowledge	Shakespeare *Macbeth* AQA GCSE English Literature Paper 1 Skills and Knowledge End of Year 10 Assessments Spoken Language Assessment	
Year 11	Unseen Poetry × 4 weeks 19th Century Novel × 8 weeks *A Christmas Carol* AQA GCSE English Literature Papers 1 and 2 Skills and Knowledge Mock examinations	Revision AQA Paper 1 GCSE English Language AQA Paper 2 GCSE English Literature	Revision AQA Paper 2 GCSE English Language AQA Paper 1 GCSE English Literature Final mocks	Revision and start of final exam period Closing the final gaps	Final exam period	

Now let's take this a step further. You will notice in the first column in the task box on page 19, I have added some possible overarching themes for each year group. Through these themes, you can consolidate knowledge and generate more depth of thought for students by enabling them to make logical connections across the academic year. You can also add considerably to cultural capital by making meaningful cross-curricular links.

Before you select your overarching theme, go and have a cup of tea with the Humanities leader in your school. The National Curriculum for History and Geography does provide subject content in a more focused way than the Programme of Study for English. So what are they doing and when? How might the topics and time periods they teach enhance the teaching of certain texts and topics in English?

Now have a chat with your Drama department. (You can hopefully see there is potential for a lot of tea and cake when curriculum planning!) How can you work together so that practical drama lessons can be used to enhance the teaching of texts or build confidence in play reading, performing Shakespeare or hot-seating characters from a novel?

Task

Look at the possible overarching themes for each year group below and the possible core texts and topics that have been added as the basis for the English curriculum.

- What other texts could you add that would work well?
- What can feasibly be completed in the time?
- Can you create a balance in terms of representation across your curriculum?
- What possibilities are afforded by your choices in terms of creating breadth, challenge and diversity?
- What scope is there for developing the core skills of reading, writing and oracy?

Year and overarching theme	Autumn 1 Modern prose fiction	Autumn 2 Poetry anthologies	Spring 1 Drama text	Spring 2 19th century project	Summer 1 Shakespeare text	Summer 2 Writing
Year 7 Magical Worlds	*The Girl of Ink and Stars*				*A Midsummer Night's Dream*	Narrative writing: Adventure stories
Year 8 Conflict and Compassion		Poems of War and Refuge × 6 poems	*The Diary of Anne Frank*			
Year 9 How We Treat Others	*Noughts and Crosses*			*The Victorian City*		Persuasive writing: Protest and social justice

Many of the units in the table above have a core text or anthology of texts at their heart, thereby creating the breadth of reading demanded by the National Curriculum. My nineteenth-century projects allowed me to make use of a number of extracts from nineteenth-century texts – prose and poetry, fiction and non-fiction – to broaden experience in a manageable way. I was lucky enough to be able to develop this project-based learning idea into *Reimagine Key Stage 3 English* for Collins. By curating the schemes of work around these texts or topic areas, it is possible to embed developmental work on reading comprehension, work on analysis of language and creative and transactional writing opportunities, all of which lead us seamlessly towards GCSE assessment objectives.

Equally, by clearly embedding logical and simple-to-follow methods throughout Key Stage 3, methods that are followed by all of the department in synchronicity, students are able to step into Key Stage 4 with a developed toolkit of skills and knowledge firmly embedded. In this way, as practitioners, we can focus on actually enjoying our GCSE courses instead of trying to get students to start from scratch on very basic skills. In Chapter 2 we will begin to explore how this might work in practice.

Strategies and takeaways

- **Get the full picture:** Create a five-year curriculum which makes use of vertical threads from Years 7 to 11.
- **Add warp to the weft:** Create an overarching theme for each year of Key Stage 3 to aid deeper and more critical thinking and conceptualisation of ideas, linking texts and topics by theme.
- **Less is more:** Consider the feasibility of what you can teach in the timeframes you have. Don't make it a continuous sprint for your students and your team with no time to embed and consolidate learning.

Chapter 2: The Spiral Curriculum

What is the vertical spiral?

Looking back at our potential five-year plan for teaching GCSE English Language and English Literature, it's time to consider why we might want to place the study of particular genres and topics all in the same half term for each year group.

By ensuring each term or half term focuses on a specific genre – for example modern prose fiction or Shakespeare – we create a seamless spiral through Years 7–9, developing knowledge and the ability to apply that knowledge with increasing complexity and sophistication in terms of reading, writing, speaking and listening.

Consider, for example, the study of prose fiction. In teaching a class reader, we are going to spend much of our time on comprehension work and skills. Doubtless, we will do many other things too – exploring language, using the text as a stimulus for creative writing, and so on. But much of our focus is likely to be on ideas, inferential reading, exploring themes and characters, and the importance of places.

When we teach a unit of poetry, though of course we will explore ideas and themes here too, we are more likely to weight the content of our teaching towards exploring language: choices of vocabulary and phrases, the creation of imagery, the structure and shape of the poems we work with and their effect and impact.

When we move on in later terms to teach a modern drama or a Shakespeare play, we are probably going to introduce more oracy into our classroom through reading aloud; we are going to introduce vocabulary related to theatre and dramatic conventions; and we may consider a play in performance perhaps, alongside the inferential reading and literary analysis.

We can see, therefore, how logical this skills and knowledge building might be on a typical horizontal plane.

	Autumn 1 Modern prose fiction 8 weeks	Autumn 2 Poetry anthologies 4 weeks	Spring 1 Drama text 6 weeks	Spring 2 19th century project 6 weeks	Summer 1 and 2 Shakespeare text Writing 8 weeks + 3 weeks + Assessment week	
Year 7 Magical Worlds	*The Girl of Ink and Stars*	Poems of Magic and Adventure	*Treasure Island* playscript	The Natural World	*A Midsummer Night's Dream*	Narrative writing: Adventure stories

But how about the vertical plane?

	Autumn 1 Modern prose fiction	Autumn 2 Poetry anthologies
Year 7 Magical Worlds	*The Girl of Ink and Stars*	Poems of Magic and Adventure
Year 8 Conflict and Compassion	*The Book Thief*	Poems of War and Refuge
Year 9 How We Treat Others	*Noughts and Crosses*	Poems of Love and Identity
Year 10	20th and 21st Century Fiction AQA GCSE English Language Paper 1 Skills and Knowledge Narrative Writing	Poems of Power and Conflict AQA GCSE English Literature Paper 2 Skills and Knowledge Descriptive Writing
Year 11	Unseen Poetry × 4 weeks 19th Century Novel × 8 weeks *A Christmas Carol* AQA GCSE English Literature Papers 1 and 2 Skills and Knowledge Mock examinations	

If we look vertically through the five-year plan, we have the potential to create a seamless sequence of stepping-stones for the core skills, whereby a baseline is embedded for all our students year on year. And let's not make that baseline unrealistic.

Consider if, in the teaching of prose fiction in Autumn 1, we included working on comprehension skills with all students as part of our scheme of work. I long ago dispensed with the old PEE/PEA (Point-Evidence-Explanation/Analysis) method for comprehension – more of that in Chapter 5 – so in teaching comprehension my goal was for all students to be able to make a very clear statement which addressed the focus of the question, to support that statement with an appropriate quotation from our chosen text and be able to draw out an inference from that quotation to show their understanding. Some of my Year 7s could do that. Many could not, or at least not with any real clarity, or without resorting to paraphrasing.

However, imagine if we introduced that method in Year 7, continued to push for it in Year 8 and aimed to secure it for everyone by Year 9. By the end of working on the class reader, while not every child in Year 7 would have super sparkly polished comprehension skills, might it be feasible to ensure *every* child could make that sensible clear statement in response to a task, preventing them from launching straight into quotations that may or may not be helpful and encouraging them to be more thoughtful and selective about their choice of supporting references? This approach allows us to develop vocabulary too, in considering how we might describe the character or place referred to in the question, to show more knowledge and aid precision. So, for example, in Year 7 I would suggest framing comprehension questions using 'what' and encouraging inference in the statement response through keywords such as 'learn', 'understand', 'infer' or 'imply'.

> ### What do we learn about the character of Maia?
> Maia is brave and fearless when she sets out in the boat.
> ### What do we understand about the island the children have landed on?
> The island is dark, unwelcoming and covered in trees.
> ### What is implied about the house in the forest?
> The house seems like it is deserted and neglected.

By the end of Year 8, might it be feasible for *all* students to be able to make clear statements of response, followed by relevant supporting quotations?

> ### What do we learn about the green jug?
> We learn that the green jug had been made by Isabella's mother and was precious to the family: 'Da kept it out of reach and washed it with great care.'
> The jug was the last thing Isabella's mother made before her death and was kept for special occasions: 'We only used it on the first day of school... feast days.'

Many students will, by this stage, be able to go on and draw out interesting inferences of course. But what if, by the end of Year 9, every student was able to draw out a clear and sensible inference and present it methodically?

> **What do we learn about Kairos City from the opening chapters?**
> We learn that Kairos City is a place where people have different
> labels: 'What must it be like... to peer into the lives of Paragons.'
> This suggests that the citizens there are not equal and have
> different levels of wealth and privilege.
> We also learn that Kairos City has no natural features, as it says
> 'A screen announced the sickly scent to be Essence of Forest Glade'.
> This implies that its people are prevented from enjoying nature
> and live in a place which is soulless and false.

By making this skill our key indicator of progress for every student, would that not help us to deal very swiftly and easily with AO1 tasks at GCSE, particularly in some specifications where they may have to do this with more than one text?

Here's an example AO1 GCSE English Language exam-style question:

READING (50%)	
Read and understand a range of texts to:	
AO1	• Identify and interpret explicit and implicit information and ideas
	• Select and synthesise evidence from different texts

> **Both writers describe an encounter with living creatures.**
> **Use details from both sources to write a summary of the**
> **similarities between the creatures they encounter.**
> Both writers have encounters with living creatures that are
> extremely large. In source A, we learn the creature 'is magnificent'
> and 'enormous'. In source B, we learn the tortoises 'must have
> weighed at least two hundred pounds'. This suggests that the
> creatures were an impressive sight and their sheer size and scale
> was the first thing both writers were drawn to.

Discussing this approach with a department I was working with, the Head of English commented: 'At first, I was thinking that this was just too simple to set as a target for the year group, but the more I thought about it, the more I realised we are still going back and teaching them basic comprehension and how to select quotations in Year 11. This would totally solve that.'

Less is more

I mentioned in Chapter 1 how some Key Stage 3 curriculum plans can look extremely ambitious and overloaded. Don't get me wrong: I'm all for ambition and breadth and challenge. But I do think we have to guard against throwing huge amounts of content at students and hoping some of it will stick. I'm a firm believer in getting the basics right.

Is there any point in listing three dozen linguistic terms on your curriculum map, that students must know by the end of Year 8, if they still can't tell an adverb from an adjective and don't have the foggiest idea about how to comment on the effect of a simple simile? Less is always more; add to the spiral step-by-step.

A cursory glance at the appendices for English at Key Stage 2 might suggest that all of our students will come to us in Year 7 with something close to a degree in linguistics. This is clearly not the case. I've taught some very able Year 7 students indeed in my thirty-year career, but not one of them has ever invited me into a discussion about the passive tense or what degree of possibility they might convey in a sentence through a pertinent choice of modal verb. Those students may well be out there, but we may also have students with reading ages much lower than their chronological age; students who have second or additional languages; students who may not have attended Year 6 at all through illness; or students who have just arrived in the UK and have had to enter a whole new life and system of schooling.

Working with poetry is a fantastic way to add to our spiral curriculum by introducing and developing a knowledge bank of key subject terminology in a way that can be joyful and imaginative. Poetry is an area of the English curriculum that students often find difficult, and then what becomes the default position? Poetry is boring. How many times have we heard that as English teachers, and then died a little inside? Though, to be honest, I've died a little more when I've heard 'I hate teaching poetry' when delivering CPD to teachers!

A thoughtfully curated selection of perhaps six poems covered over a half term or block of four weeks can deliver in spades. Consider using the poetry unit in Year 7 to embed a very basic toolkit of subject terminology while creatively exploring the ideas and themes of your chosen poems. Imagine if all of our Year 7s could recognise aspects of language such as adjectives, noun phrases, similes and metaphors; then simple aspects of structure such as the use of stanzas, repetition and rhyming couplets. By reinforcing and making realistic additions to that toolkit in Year 8 and then Year 9, wouldn't that enable all of our students to achieve at least some marks for AO2 questions at GCSE? If, by Year 8, we could enable all of our students to make some sensible and clear comments on the effect of those features they can correctly identify, we would be on a great journey into AO2. Perhaps by Year 9 we could then introduce some simple comparisons between poems...

Most Principal Examiners' reports into English Literature each year make a mention of subject terminology, with the key message being that there is no need for students to use elaborate terms. In fact, the use of the flashy term is very often unconvincing and (though it won't say this in the report) quite annoying.

There's no real mileage in students using obscure terminology if the examiner reading the work has to look it up to decide if it's a feature of language or a dinosaur, particularly if the candidate has got muddled up between anadiplosis and diplodocus. (Believe me, I've seen it all.) It flatters to deceive, particularly if the candidate is then unable to convincingly comment on its effect or impact.

Knowing linguistic terminology is a shorthand, a code, for being able to pinpoint particular aspects of language or structure. For example, it's very useful to know what a metaphor is when you are trying to explain the effect of, 'It is the East, and Juliet is the sun', rather than having to say, 'Shakespeare says Juliet is something she isn't, so we compare her to it in our mind's eye':

> Shakespeare uses a metaphor, 'It is the East, and Juliet is the sun', to make us see how Romeo views Juliet as being something celestial, a source of light and warmth.

Reflection

Consider how many times you have corrected simple mistakes in terminology over the course of your teaching, and how many times you are still seeing those simple mistakes in mock examination papers.

What would a 'less is more' approach, with clear room to embed that core knowledge and key skills, look like in your curriculum?

The five stages of the journey

Developing a spiral curriculum provides opportunities to work at those key elements of the subject. For example, introducing and developing comprehension skills, then securing our students' ability to read texts with increasing understanding, supporting ideas, and making increasingly perceptive inferences and critical judgements. The spiral provides the chance to build students' knowledge around the language of texts, thus boosting their own vocabulary and encouraging them to foster a love of language and its possibilities. Ultimately, this leads to a confident ability to analyse and explore language effects, in readiness for GCSE study and beyond. It offers the chance to gradually build a knowledge of how texts are structured and how this more challenging concept can help us to formulate readings and meanings with more sophistication.

This knowledge, in turn, can be translated into a means of developing students' own writing and expression with opportunities to engage in meaningful writing activities, thus creating secure and confident communicators of the future. Placing specific writing modules in your spiral plan will enable an in-depth study of writing to increase knowledge of planning, accuracy, complex grammatical constructs and punctuation for impact and effect. Though I would encourage writing responses as creative outcomes for all textual study throughout the year, you will notice my specific assessed units on this are placed in half term 6, to allow students to explore the craft of writing more fully using the reading experiences of the academic year.

This approach allows you to provide a rich, challenging yet realistic programme of study that enables students to build their subject knowledge and apply that knowledge skilfully via a spiral curriculum which provides a logical progression through their five-year study. We can now begin to see that the curriculum moves through five stages:

- Introducing
- Developing
- Securing
- Expanding
- Perfecting.

And with each stage, the core elements of the English curriculum gain in strength and momentum. You'll notice I've not included the word 'mastering' in that list. Call me an old-fashioned sort of feminist, but I have issues with that word. It always makes me recall one of my own privileges as a trainee English teacher when I was lucky enough to sit in on a lecture given by Professor Angela Goddard on language and gender. She asked us to reflect on the sentence: 'We found the Old Master in the attic' and then substitute the word 'mistress' for 'master'. Interesting difference. I never forgot that English lecture.

So, I can't subscribe to the verb 'to master' given both its patriarchal and colonial connotations.

Let's look at how each of the five stages can be applied to Years 7–11 in the spiral curriculum plan below:

	Autumn 1 Modern prose fiction × 8 weeks	Autumn 2 Poetry anthologies × 4 weeks
Year 7: Introducing Magical Worlds	*The Girl of Ink and Stars* Kiran Millwood Hargrave	Poems of Magic and Adventure
Year 8: Developing Conflict and Compassion	*The Book Thief* Markus Zusak	Poems of War and Refuge
Year 9: Securing How We Treat Others	*Noughts and Crosses* Malorie Blackman	Poems of Love and Identity
Year 10: Expanding	20th and 21st Century Fiction AQA GCSE English Language Paper 1 Skills and Knowledge Narrative Writing	Poems of Power and Conflict AQA GCSE English Literature Paper 2 Skills and Knowledge Descriptive Writing
Year 11: Perfecting	Unseen Poetry × 4 weeks 19th Century Novel × 8 weeks *A Christmas Carol* AQA GCSE English Literature Papers 1 and 2 Skills and Knowledge Mock examinations	

Task

Take some time to reflect on this idea and curate a brief 'wish list' of skills in the table below.

Keep it simple. Keep it realistic. Less is more.

Wouldn't it be great if by the end of Year 7 every student could:	Wouldn't it be brilliant if by the end of Year 8 every student could:	Wouldn't it be fantastic if by the end of Year 9 every student could:	That would mean that when we move to GCSE, all students would be secure in:

Key Progress Indicators

Introducing this learning spiral with my own department, I moved on to consider how we might track this progress. I could, of course, generate yet another spreadsheet of doom for my team, but I wanted to introduce a system where the students themselves were able to feel a sense of achievement and could see themselves moving to a position of conscious competence through Key Stage 3, so that their skills and knowledge were second nature by Key Stage 4.

Beginning with your plan for the scheme of work to be covered in each half term, ask a simple question: 'What is the *one thing* out of the work we cover each week of the scheme that we want every student to have understood and/or learned how to do?'

From this, a sequence of Key Progress Indicators, or KPIs, can be created. These are not as fancy or as complicated as they sound. Rather, they could boil down as follows:

- What are we teaching in half term 1 of Year 7/8/9?
- What are we going to be doing in Week 1 of the curriculum? (This would be the third week of Year 7 if you've done the observation and information gathering weeks discussed in Chapter 1.)
- What one thing do we want everyone to have grasped in Week 1, and so on, through the term or half term?

These key areas of learning can then be built into the department's week-by-week plans and schemes of work. Again, the focus should be on keeping these simple so that they are achievable for all students in varying degrees. A simple checklist for students in their exercise books at the start of each term can help them reflect on what they have achieved or are on the way to achieving each week, and enable them to engage in a dialogue with their teacher in a secure way. That level of achievement will then be reflected through a completed task or tasks from that week's work.

Across the term in Year 7 above, we might have begun the year with our observation phase. Then, moving into the study of the class reader, we might have included any number of activities in our first week of reading. However, the key thing we want everyone to be able to do in Week 1 is complete some accurate retrieval and be able to express their ideas in clear statement sentences.

For example, a possible checklist of the key aspects of skills and knowledge for Year 7 in Term 1 might look a little something like this:

Year 7 Term 1 KPIs	Comment	How well do I understand this skill? 😊😐☹️
7:1:1 Be able to retrieve basic ideas/info from a modern prose text and make statements		
7:1:2 Begin to support statements with quotations		
7:1:3 Be able to attempt inferences from our reading		
7:1:4 Know and use adjectives when describing a character		
7:1:5 Recognise and explore similes in our class reader		
7.1.6 Plan and write a description of a place in our class reader using adjectives and similes		
7:1:7 Recognise and begin to comment on basic descriptive language features/imagery in poetry (adjective, simile, metaphor, personification)		
7:1:8 Recognise and begin to comment on basic structural features in poetry (repetition, stanza, rhyme, patterns of alliteration)		

Over Weeks 2 and 3, as well as reading, talking together and exploring ideas, we might want to introduce the idea of quotations and how to use these to support our ideas. We might want to demonstrate how to 'explode' quotations and begin to think about inferences. Not every student will be able to demonstrate that on paper, but they will at least have begun their journey.

That journey will take them on the horizontal plane through Year 7, but it will also take students on the vertical plane through Year 8 and into Year 9 where core skills and knowledge can be consolidated and secured before moving into the Expanding phase of Year 10 and the demands of an examination syllabus.

Here's how the week-by-week student checklist might look for the same term in Year 9:

Year 9 Term 1 KPIs	Comment	How well do I understand this skill? ☺ 😐 ☹
9:1:1 Use our statement/quotation/inference method confidently to create longer answers		
9:1:2 Know and understand the use of language features in prose fiction (adjective, adverb, metaphor, simile, alliteration, personification, onomatopoeia, etc.)		
9:1:3 Understand how a theme develops in a prose fiction text		
9.1:4 Understand how to empathise with a character and present our thoughts and feelings in a diary response		
9:1:5 Understand how the 5-point narrative structure works and use this to plan our own narratives		
9:1:6 Plan and write a sustained, structured narrative		
9.1:7 Know and understand our identify/example/comment method for analytical work on poetry		
9.1:8 Know and understand structural features in prose and poetry (contrast, time, tense, sentence structures, stanza, rhyme, rhythm, repetition, etc.)		
9.1:9 Understand how to make comparative links with both poetry and prose texts		

One of the key benefits of this simple system is that it can help us as practitioners to identify misconceptions and gaps in learning very quickly. Looking back over the lessons of any given week, I could take a little reflection time with students (often in the last lesson of the week) and ask them to complete their comment boxes before taking in their books to mark and offer feedback on that week's work. If someone had been absent, we could use that time to ensure they had the relevant materials. If someone had not understood or felt they had not grasped an aspect of knowledge or a concept, they could jot it in their comments privately for me. The simple emojis were actually more telling than one might think as to a student's level of confidence. Students were surprisingly honest – even Year 9s – and a sad face meant I needed to offer a little more support or give more help in a particular area to a specific student. In turn, this approach makes it possible for you to close gaps in learning much more quickly and be much more responsive than waiting for the data from a midterm test, for example.

If you are leading a department, another key benefit of this approach is that it can ensure that all of your team are embedding core skills and knowledge consistently across each year group. Working with KPIs as part of your planning and delivery helps you to ensure that all of the students you have responsibility for as a leader have access to the same learning journey and are working in logical stepping-stones towards a shared end goal. It can help to ensure that a consistent pace of learning is maintained across all of your teaching groups so that no one group is left behind or misses out on a key aspect of the curriculum. It can help to create structure and continuity if you have staffing changes or need to use cover or supply staff. When you do a book scrutiny, examining selections of students' work from across a year group, it can also help you to identify where additional support or CPD is needed. A lot of puzzled or sad face emojis for the drama unit? Maybe your trainee or early career teacher is less confident with that text and could use a little extra support or subject knowledge enhancement.

Reflection

Reflect on the examples of possible KPI checklists on pages 29–31 for Year 7 and Year 9.

- How do they show progression in the core skills and knowledge that can be acquired through the study of a class reader and selection of poetry in Autumn half terms 1 and 2?

- If this was the baseline of content, might it be feasible to expect every student to hit those milestones to some degree?

- How might this spiral of skills and knowledge help to prepare students for the first term of Year 10 (shown in the grid on page 28)?

Task

Imagine you are planning to teach a Shakespeare play across eight weeks in Term 3 for Year 7 at Key Stage 3. How might you develop a set of KPIs to do that across the eight weeks?

- Choose a play you know well and draft the core skills and knowledge you would want your Year 7 students to acquire by the end of the eight-week study.
- Consider the kinds of activities your students might complete across the scheme of work: what possible skills and knowledge could you embed as the weeks progress?
- Finally, evaluate how you might layer up those skills through Years 8 and 9 to make stepping into the GCSE English Literature Shakespeare text and the demands of its assessment much more seamless and accessible.

Year 7 Term 3 KPIs Weeks 1–8 Text:
7:3:1
7:3:2
7:3:3
7:3:4
7:3:5
7.:3:6
7:3:7
7:3:8

Strategies and takeaways

- **Make the wish list:** Establish a baseline of skills and knowledge which could be taught through each term for each year group of Key Stage 3 through your chosen genres/choices of texts and/or topics.
- **Keep it real:** Keep that baseline of skills and knowledge feasible. Continuously ask yourself if every student would be able to achieve those skills to some degree.
- **Stepping up:** Visualise the trajectory of skills through the three years of Key Stage 3 and feeding into the Expanding and Perfecting stages of Key Stage 4.
- **Join the dots:** Build those skills into your midterm and week-by-week plans and schemes of work. (More on this in Chapter 4.)
- **See the journey ahead:** Create Key Progress Indicators for students to help them see and visualise their learning progress and encourage dialogue with you.

Chapter 3: Text Choices with Soul

What are you reading?

One of the biggest decisions to make when planning our English curriculum, and one that warrants very careful thought and consideration, is the choice of texts we might use as the building blocks for this.

Much emphasis has been placed, in recent years, on two particular issues: increasing cultural capital for students and increasing the diversity of the texts we study. I would suggest that if an English curriculum has been well-planned and is broad and balanced, has its finger on the pulse (i.e. hasn't nodded off in a dusty stockroom!) and is taught by knowledgeable and passionate practitioners then, by default, it cannot help but broaden students' experiences, raise their awareness, facilitate fantastic outcomes and enrich their soul.

However, in many cases, despite my firm conviction that English teachers are a wild and crazy bunch, the experience of English for many students in school has been anything but wild and crazy. We have seen the uptake of English at A Level in all its forms decrease significantly in recent years and this has been reported with concern by organisations such as The National Association for the Teaching of English (NATE), The English Association and The English and Media Centre. This has seemingly led to reductions in numbers in those opting to study English in higher education, followed by news of devastating cuts in university departments. Though other factors, such as the championing of STEM subjects, have surely contributed to this decline, the experience that students have of the subject needs critical and urgent examination. Our choices, therefore, as curators of the English curriculum in secondary schools, have consequences, and they extend much more widely than the percentages of Grades 5 and above achieved each year.

I was having a coffee with a brilliant colleague recently. She was taking up a post in an all-boys school, where results had to make a significant improvement: 'Before I say anything Jo, just have a look at this curriculum map they have been following and tell me honestly what you think...'. As experienced English teachers and inferential readers you can probably tell where this was going. The English plan my colleague had inherited – and thankfully was about to radically change – could have been written in the 1920s rather than the 2020s. It was a boys' school, yes, but no one seemed to have even heard of women. There were no women authors. There were no writers of colour. There was absolutely nothing contemporary in any of the text choices: the diet was Shakespeare and the nineteenth century.

And this is not unusual.

I worked with an amazing department some time ago to look at their Key Stage 3 curriculum, which was packed to the gills with lots of lovely ideas of what to *do* with texts. However, my first observation was that all of the texts studied in Years 7 and 9 were by authors who were male and White. Add that to the GCSE choices and it compounds an unbalanced offering.

A multi-academy trust I know of rolled out its definitive Key Stage 3 English curriculum recently. And yet, every author was White and male. This is in a trust where a large proportion of its schools are in cities that are richly and vibrantly multicultural. Only one text was from the twenty-first century and that was designated for Year 7 midway through the year. This was a challenging read that I felt many Year 7s would struggle with. I mentioned in Chapter 1 how important it is to ascertain just where our students are at when they join us in Year 7. We have routinely heard in recent years of Year 7s arriving in secondary schools with reading ages far below their chronological age. How will we ever foster a love of reading and a desire to read in those 11-year-olds if we give them a diet that is as undigestible, unpalatable and difficult to wade through as the slimy cabbage that was piled on my plate for 1970s school dinners under the pretext of being good for me?

I would suggest we need to guard a little against intellectual snobbery too. Have we fallen into an Orwellian trap, as a profession, of thinking 'old texts good; new texts bad'? Is it perhaps possible that some of the amazing Young Adult (YA) fiction that is available to us today has been marginalised in favour of material that is perceived to be 'high quality' because of its vintage? And if so, how do we reconcile that against one of the outcomes of the Teach First 'Missing Pages' report in September 2020 which found that:

> ❛75% of English teachers had concerns about a lack of ethnic diversity in the curriculum and 98% felt it important to include ethnic minority authors in the secondary English curriculum?❜

It is worth reminding ourselves that what has traditionally been considered 'high-quality' literature and therefore ascribed to 'the canon' has social and political implications way beyond those of making textual choices. The authors of *Rewriting English: Cultural Politics of Gender and Class* comment that the whole construct of canon formation was developed: 'in the establishment of curriculum for imperial dominations. For "English Literature" was born, as a school and college subject, not in England but in the mission schools and training colleges of Africa and India' (Batsleer et al. 2003, p.23). There's an interesting thought to look at through a post-colonial lens and is perhaps a PhD topic for another day.

So where do we begin with our choices in our departments?

Let's begin with you. Take a moment to be nostalgic and reminisce about the texts you read and studied in secondary school and for your examinations. At what point did you begin to love the subject so much you wanted to devote your professional life to it? Was it one particular novel, a beautiful poem, reading a play around the class? Maybe you had an inspirational teacher, but which text did they bring to life for you so vividly that you chose to continue studying this subject, our subject, in particular? Then: at university. What kind of texts did you experience? Did you feel that you had access to and experience of a broad enough range of texts to make you feel you have sufficient expertise and confidence to teach more diverse text choices now?

And what about your own bookshelf? Go on, grab a coffee and have a rifle through it. What is on your own bookshelf and your bedside table right here and now (apart, of course, from this juicy little offering)? What are you reading for pleasure? Have a think about the last book you bought or read by an author from a different culture or faith, gender or sexuality, ethnicity or even age from yourself. We might stop to consider how we feel when we, as expert readers, become open to new experiences or perspectives through our reading, or recognise that one of our unconscious biases has been addressed. Perhaps there was a time when you saw yourself represented in a text in a way you hadn't before. We could all probably cite any number of texts that, over our reading history, have made an impact on us – and this is what perpetuates our love of reading.

I can remember vividly the experience of reading *Catch-22* for the first time as an A-Level student. I remember a poem by C. P. Cavafy that my A-Level teacher had distributed on Valentine's Day that stayed on my bedroom wall all through my university days. I remember my tutor on my Women's Writing option at university teaching *Oranges Are Not the Only Fruit* – at the time only recently published – and beginning my lifelong fangirl love of Jeanette Winterson. I remember reading Richard Wright's *Native Son* in one sitting until four in the morning because even though I could predict its tragic ending, I couldn't leave the protagonist. My American Novel course also meant that *Gatsby* has been my all-time favourite novel to teach for A Level over the years. Last summer, I sat in sunshine and read *Open Water* by Caleb Azumah Nelson which won the Costa First Novel Award in 2021. It had the same profound effect on me as the first time I read *Gatsby* and I wished I was in a place where I could teach the texts together to A-Level students, such was the beauty and originality of its prose.

So, how are we going to foster that love in our students, year after year, in our own English departments and faculties? Are we feeding them a diet to nourish their souls or kill their desire to read stone-dead? A colleague whom I collaborated with on teaching resources for diverse texts for Key Stages 3 and 4 often cites a useful adage based on her own reading experiences in school: 'you cannot be what you cannot see.' It is worth reflecting that the choices of texts we present to our students will not only affect their desire to read creatively but also to write creatively: our future wordsmiths, poets, playwrights, novelists, journalists lie in your hands.

Task

Looking at your own curriculum maps across the five years (or seven years if you have Sixth Form), collate the authors that are currently studied into the table below. Don't worry about every extract you use: think about the main text coverage.

Text audit	Poets	Dramatists	Novelists/ short-story writers	Non-fiction writers/ journalists
Year 7				
Year 8				
Year 9				
Year 10				
Year 11				
Year 12 if applicable				
Year 13 if applicable				

Then evaluate:

- What is the balance between contemporary and 'classic' texts across the five years?
- What is the balance between contemporary texts, nineteenth century and Shakespeare?
- What gender balance do you see?
- How representative are the text choices of the students that make up the school community? What texts do you have on the curriculum from writers of colour or LGBTQ+ writers?

The perception of narrowness

Many practitioners and commentators feel very strongly that the text choices within the English curriculum have become narrower since GCSE reform happened and new specifications were launched in 2015. This is an interesting perspective. Prior to reform, there was political concern that text choices for GCSE Literature had become very narrow indeed and that the vast majority of GCSE students – no matter their ability – were studying *Of Mice and Men* and very little else. It seems somewhat ironic that a political move to broaden the English curriculum has led to perceptions that it has become narrower.

Perhaps what we mean is that the balance of texts changed.

In his journal article, 'Changes to the English Literature GCSE: A Sociocultural Perspective', Adam Morby (2014) creates a useful table illustrating this shift across four major examination boards:

	AQA		OCR		EdEXCEL		WJEC	
	2015	2017	2015	2017	2015	2017	2015	2017
Modern texts (post-1917)	40%	20%	50%	25%	50%	25%	41%	20%
Literary heritage and poetry (pre-1917)	60%	80%	50%	75%	50%	75%	59%	80%

An increased requirement for students to cover complete texts and poetry from the nineteenth century meant that examination boards had to make text choices that were accessible to GCSE students while not depleting the choices available for A-Level study. As we might expect, similar choices emerged from all the major examination boards, with *Dr Jekyll and Mr Hyde* and *A Christmas Carol* coming out as hot (and short!) favourites.

As a former Principal Examiner for GCSE English Language, I trained many thousands of teachers in the requirements of the new specification. One of the real concerns that I encountered from colleagues was anxiety surrounding nineteenth-century texts – not just the teaching of a full text for Literature but the requirement for GCSE students to face unseen material from the nineteenth century as part of their terminal examination in English Language: a requirement interestingly not extended to the IGCSE specifications favoured by many independent and prestigious public schools.

This anxiety, perhaps, has fuelled the desire to introduce more nineteenth-century texts at Key Stage 3. On the surface, this seems like a good plan. However, we also have to weigh this against the reading ages, fluency and ability of our students as well as the need to engage them in the subject. Have we now got the majority of Year 7 students ploughing through *Oliver Twist* in the same way that almost every Year 11 student had *Of Mice and Men* in their bag a decade ago?

Gradually introducing students to nineteenth-century texts and themes was my own way of dealing with this. I introduced project-based learning into my classroom, building confidence with extracts from key novels, poems and non-fiction texts with thematic links rather than expecting them to study whole texts – which would also mean a more limited experience in terms of possible range. I would then interleave comprehension work and analysis of those texts with creative and transactional writing opportunities. This meant I could familiarise students with the language and themes of nineteenth-century texts in an engaging and palatable way while managing the reading challenge for them. I was lucky enough to have the opportunity to develop and edit these projects into a published resource as *Reimagine Key Stage 3 English* (Heathcote et al. 2020).

I scheduled my project-based nineteenth-century work part way through the year – once students had had some experience of modern prose fiction and a range of poetry, and before they tackled a Shakespeare text. This meant I could begin the year with a work of modern prose fiction as a class reader. You will have seen from examples in Chapters 1 and 2 that each year of the possible Key Stage 3 curriculum plan begins with a work of modern prose fiction. My reasons for that are very clear. I wanted to start the year with a solid unit of work, where I could work on basic comprehension skills with Year 7 and then develop and secure those through Years 8 and 9. A shared class reading experience can bond the group, allowing for much discussion, speculation, inference and prediction. Making a good choice here is a good 'buy in' for student engagement and investment in the characters, plot and themes. It allows close-up work on writers' methods to put some building blocks in place before a study of poetry. It stimulates creative writing, allowing you to complete formative assessment right across the skills range. It leads directly into core GCSE English Language and Literature studies in Years 10 and 11.

Most importantly, a modern prose text is an opportunity for students to read something they can access and understand collectively, and at Key Stage 3 it is one of your best opportunities for diversifying your curriculum and introducing relatively new and fresh writing into your classroom. There are no limitations or restrictions on what we could choose here.

Increasing diversity and representation

Looking back to Adam Morby's findings, the coverage of modern texts halved across all of the major specifications in order to meet the requirements of the 2015 reform. However, it is very interesting to note that in this component – where there was much more scope for a broad range of diverse cultures and identities to be represented – many old favourites remained on the set text list: *An Inspector Calls*, *Animal Farm*, *Lord of the Flies*. This would, of course, keep teachers and departments – perhaps working within limited budgets to buy in new texts – happy.

For many years I worked with and was mentored by a highly inspirational and charismatic Chief Examiner. He held some strong opinions and taught me to value my own. One of his was that the very last people you should ask about text choices for a new specification were teachers. When I asked him why he thought this he suggested that teachers want to teach what they know and are familiar with. He wasn't being disparaging here. As practitioners, we are so busy that any change adds to workload, adds to pressure, adds to stress levels and costs yet more time in an already up-to-and-beyond-capacity schedule. It is interesting that, under my colleague's tenure as Chief Examiner, we were teaching an anthology of poetry from a wide variety of cultures and traditions – a choice that seemed daunting to many practitioners at its inception with texts in patois and including Gujarati script, and yet became very popular with students and teachers over time. It was lovely to teach and was lost during reform.

Task

Poetry is an amazing way to increase the diversity and representation across your curriculum. Think back to the plans created in Chapter 1 for the spiral curriculum. My overarching themes were: Magical Worlds; Conflict and Compassion; How We Treat Others.

What overarching themes might you wish to use in your own curriculum? Add them to the table below and then create a 'wish list' of possible poems you could use to curate an exciting anthology for each year group. Aim to browse and select approximately six poems for each anthology. Consider a representative mix of identities across your selection. Aim to include poets who are new to you too.

Overarching theme: Year 7 selection	
Overarching theme: Year 8 selection	
Overarching theme: Year 9 selection	

Following reform, newer and more diverse choices remained thin on the ground. Out of all the possible works of prose fiction by brilliant women writers of colour that were available, three major examination specifications selected Meera Syal's *Anita and Me*. It's a very funny, heart-warming and beautifully written novel that I have used in class many times. But it's odd to me that we would see it across three specifications for three separate boards: unimaginative almost.

Of course, we are now almost a decade on from reformed specifications and we are a few years down the line from the publication of the 'Missing Pages' report, which highlighted:

> ❛ that the biggest exam board, accounting for almost 80% of GCSE English literature entries, did not feature a single book by a Black author, and just two books by ethnic minority authors. ❜

More recently, we have seen moves to refresh the set text choices for GCSE Literature to create a more diverse curriculum where there is scope to do so, i.e. within Modern Texts and Poetry. Exam boards are now 'refreshing' anthologies with more varied choices that were ironically there in some legacy specifications. While new inclusions are to be welcomed, it is noteworthy that the texts being replaced have included 'less popular' choices such as *Never Let Me Go* by Japanese-British writer Kazuo Ishiguro and the playscript of *The Curious Incident of the Dog in the Night-Time* which deals so powerfully with the issues and feelings of a neurodiverse central character.

The fact that those choices are less popular is somewhat ironic to be sure. Indeed, even *Anita and Me* had very little take-up across all of the specifications, signalling perhaps that the mere presence of a text by a writer of colour on a set list isn't enough to move teachers away from the legacy texts they are comfortable and confident with.

Task

Explore the possibilities for introducing three new prose texts to begin each year of Key Stage 3. Where should you start?

- Investigate the reading lists provided online by the Book Trust, which allow you to search by age and category. The recommendations in the themed booklists are especially useful for increasing the diversity and representation of your choices.
- Go and spend an hour or so browsing the amazing YA fiction on offer in a bookshop or store which has a good selection. Although a number of established booksellers also helpfully organise YA fiction on their websites to help you increase representation and find exciting new texts, for me, an hour in a bookshop – especially one where I can sit down with a coffee – is always a treat. It's wonderful to see how publishing for this market has flourished.

Constraints and opportunities

I mentioned earlier my introduction to Winterson's *Oranges Are Not the Only Fruit* during my undergraduate years in the late 1980s. Had I been a few years younger and in school then, however, it is unlikely that text would have reached me. Section 28 of the Local Government Act 1988 banned local authorities and schools from 'promoting homosexuality'. The charitable organisation Stonewall (2003) reminds us:

> *This had deprived generations of LGBT pupils the chance of seeing people like them in the books, plays, leaflets or films their schools could stock or show. Teachers weren't allowed to teach about same-sex relationships; anyone who broke the law could face disciplinary action.*
>
> The effects were devastating and have sadly proved long-lasting and research shows that anti-LGBT bullying is still widespread with more than half of pupils (52 per cent) reporting hearing homophobic slurs frequently at school. *
>
> (Stonewall School Report 2017)

The Section 28 constraints were in place for a staggering fifteen years and were only repealed in 2003 following much determined campaigning. In those intervening years, how many students who identified as LGBTQ+ did not read a single poem, story or novel in school by a writer who could potentially represent them or their feelings and experiences as they navigated their teenage years? It is also worth considering how that lack of diversity limited the reading experiences of students of English at GCSE and A Level who then may have gone on to become English teachers themselves.

It is well worth reminding ourselves, too, of how our opportunity to increase representation in our text choices – which we would now see not only as extremely important but as a right – is also a hard-won privilege which we must not take for granted and which we should be enjoying, embracing and maximising.

It is notable, too, that change, like peace, comes 'dropping slow' as Yeats would have it. 'Missing Pages' flagged in 2020 the lack of representation of writers of colour, but it will take time for that increased representation to be seen across all examination papers. There are *no* such constraints in our Key Stage 3 classrooms. Indeed, the National Curriculum *English Programmes of Study: Key Stage 3* states that our students should be:

> ❛reading a wide range of fiction and non-fiction, including in particular whole books, short stories, poems and plays with a wide coverage of genres, historical periods, forms and authors. The range will include high-quality works from:
>
> - English literature, both pre-1914 and contemporary, including prose, poetry and drama
> - Shakespeare (two plays)
> - seminal world literature.❜

Look at the freedom that gives us as practitioners. There are no set texts here. Only choices – especially now that we've reminded ourselves that 'high-quality' work is being published in the here and now, every day, by amazing novelists, story tellers, poets, spoken word artists, journalists, dramatists and wordsmiths.

Could it be that some of our constraints are self-imposed? I mentioned earlier in the chapter the pervading philosophy of 'old texts good; new texts bad'. But what about other fears? Take a moment now (or use the task on the following page) to reflect on the barriers and unconscious – or perhaps even conscious – biases we may experience within ourselves or in our departments.

Many colleagues might argue that budgetary constraints mean that they just can't introduce new set texts at GCSE, and this is a fair point. Nor does diversifying modern texts remove the necessity of teaching Shakespeare and texts from the nineteenth century. But perhaps we can change our mindset here by looking for opportunities within those texts when developing schemes of work. (Development of schemes of work will be explored further in Chapter 4.)

We often refer to Shakespeare as having a universality, and productions through the centuries remind us of the timelessness of his themes. Performances and interpretations of Shakespeare allow us to constantly see the plays through a new lens. We must make our teaching of these set texts just as responsive too.

Consider these questions:

- How is our perception of the witches in *Macbeth* gendered? Though it tells us of the very real fears and superstitions of Shakespeare's audience, does it also allow us to discuss the tropes of toxic masculinity our students may find online today?
- Does the outcome of *Romeo and Juliet* allow us to explore whether everyone is free to love who they choose to love?
- How does the depiction of the rebellion in *The Sign of the Four* help us to see the injustices and exploitation of empire and why today feelings are so strongly evoked by cultural symbols linked to colonisation and empire?

And there is surely no way to teach *A Christmas Carol* and *An Inspector Calls* without considering the relevance of the wealth divide; exploitation; the demonisation of the poor; the need for kindness, compassion and empathy for others in an increasingly divided and polarised post-truth society.

Set texts are also just a part of the story. All of our GCSE English Language materials are unseen. We have no restrictions there in terms of what we might choose as unseen prose to develop students' skills. Often, the texts we see on examination papers can be disappointing, but *we* don't need to be disappointing. Selecting and curating your own anthology of short stories can be a much more interesting way of embedding skills for the prose fiction element of whichever examination syllabus you are following. Every time I get an 'ooh that would be brilliant for...' moment when I am reading a novel, I put a sticky note in the book. It's destined for a lesson plan, or a teaching resource or a textbook of the future.

Examined non-fiction means we can draw on all manner of journalism, travel writing, essays and memoirs and link those thematically to our Literature topics too, to add value.

Again, the unseen poetry component is a gift in terms of the opportunity to choose wisely and add balance and representation to your curriculum. It was so inspiring for me to hear from a younger colleague I was mentoring that he had put together a poetry anthology for his students that reflected all their different heritages through the choices of poets he had included. The impact and the conversations that sparked within his students was something that no spreadsheet can measure.

The choices of texts are out there. They are not difficult to find. Indeed, when working on two anthologies of diverse texts with my fellow writers, we had difficulty in selecting 24 texts for each anthology from the dozens and dozens we had come up with as a longlist.

Do your curriculum plan a favour and fill it with life-changing, flavoursome, inspiring, provocative, enriching texts that will feed the souls of your students. You'll see the impact in more ways than you could imagine.

Strategies and takeaways

- **Choose soul food:** Evaluate where the gaps are in your text choices to enable it to be representative and enriching for all of your students.
- **Quality assurance:** Avoid making value judgements and applying unconscious biases as to what 'high-quality' literature might mean.
- **Look through fresh lenses:** Turn perceived constraints into opportunities.

Chapter 4: The Lost Art of Lesson Planning

The benefit of bespoke planning

I entered the profession many years ago, decades even. My teacher training course, as many still do today, placed a real focus on lesson planning and the creation of your 'scheme of work'. And I loved it. When I completed my teaching practices, one of the really joyful and creative aspects of my training was dreaming up my lessons and making all the worksheets and related resources to accompany them – all without the aid of Google, or even a computer. I had a typewriter at home, a collection of felt-tipped pens and a box of coloured chalk. I kid you not.

I spent one of my teaching practices in a sixth form college. What a responsibility for someone with five weeks of training behind them – to be entrusted with two groups of twenty-five A-Level students, given six weeks to teach a text and set a coursework assignment which counted towards their grade, and mark it. On my welcome visit, I was taken by the Head of Department into an office with bookshelves crammed with sets of texts and simply asked: 'What do you fancy doing? My group could do with getting started on a novel. Janet's group should probably do a play.'

I went home on the train with copies of *Waiting for Godot* and *Mansfield Park* in my bag and a week to get ready for my six-week monumental responsibility. I could not wait to get started. I absolutely relished the chance to reread texts I loved, map out my six weeks as I'd been trained to do, write my lesson plans for the first week, create my resources and then respond from there once I'd met my students, some of whom were adult learners.

Over the years, this has been one of the favourite aspects of my role as an English practitioner: that element of creativity and being able to use my imagination and skills to bring texts and topics to life for students. I never threw any resource away and kept hard copies of everything in ring binders 'just in case' I needed it again. I always did need it again and this led to one department I worked in labelling me 'The Resource Queen'.

'I've got to teach Scene 3 this afternoon and I've got nothing. There's just been no time after parent's evening.'

'Ask Jo.'

'What on earth can I do to make the active and passive interesting?'

'Jo'll have something.'

'Has anybody even heard of this poem in this blooming anthology?'

'I bet Jo's got a worksheet on it.'

You get the picture.

Some time ago I had a brilliant phone call with an amazing deputy head who was looking to support a recently appointed Head of English to facilitate curriculum change and develop his leadership within a large department. In the course of our chat – which focused on the idea of revamping Key Stage 3 and creating new schemes of work from scratch – I used the phrase 'the lost art of lesson planning'. My client remembered that phrase when I went to visit – it had clearly resonated, and it was only on reflection that I realised how pertinent it could be.

For many colleagues, despite the fact that initial teacher training courses still place much focus on effective lesson planning, there is often little chance to actually do any. The internet is crammed full of teaching resources and possible lesson plans, knowledge organisers and PowerPoints, all with very good intentions to reduce workload. As Trusts have grown, many schools use centralised banks of resources or 'buy in' an off-the-shelf curriculum where schemes of work are pre-planned and mapped out, again with the good intentions of ensuring consistency.

However, I'm not sure those intentions are ever fully met. I have never once downloaded someone else's resource from the internet that I've felt happy to just lift and deliver. It always needs tweaking and more work to make it fit my lesson objectives or plan. In some cases, when I've been busy and turned to the internet for help for a few additional questions on a key scene or chapter of whatever text I'm teaching, I realise it's taking me longer to look for half a dozen questions than it would to write six of my own that specifically match my intent.

An off-the-shelf curriculum does not really take into account that schools and students and their needs are different. A scheme of work based around a particular text can work brilliantly in one school, but in a different area, with students of different backgrounds or genders or ethnicities or cultures or faiths, a different choice may be more impactful and fulfilling. Again, it's going to need work and adaptation.

I would also suggest that the one-size-fits-all model can never guarantee absolute consistency despite the best efforts of many teaching and learning gurus to impose dictatorial PowerPoint templates. Recently, I have observed lessons where 'The Template' has so many non-negotiables that the lesson content barely gets started before the bell rings. This causes me to question what is actually driving both the pace and content of the lesson. Do we remember our most inspirational teacher because of the kinds of lessons they delivered or because they used uniform PowerPoint slides?

So much of what makes a lesson comes from the delivery, from the teacher themselves, from their experience or personal style. But also, I believe, from their ownership and creative input into the curriculum and schemes of work. To stymie that passion and creative spirit in English seems almost criminal. It is a thief of joy in the English classroom and in our working lives. And, aside from anything else, it deskills the profession. It leaves us in a place where lesson planning is a lost art.

What makes a cohesive scheme of work?

Whenever I begin to work with a department on a curriculum, the first things I ask for are some large sheets of paper and marker pens. I'm a very firm believer in grasping the big picture first. In Chapter 1 we looked at creating a cohesive overview of a curriculum in; the same principles can be applied to a scheme of work.

School terms are very handily divided up into half terms, and those half terms are usually six or seven weeks long. This means we can plan very logical schemes of work which fit into those blocks of time and are punctuated by those optimistically named weeks 'the school holidays'.

Much of our work at Key Stage 3 is centred around textual study. Of course, some of our texts are longer than others. We may choose to spend an entire term on a Shakespeare text, spreading the reading load over a twelve-week period and interleaving tasks and activities to broaden the experience: using the text for reading activities, writing activities and drama. A class reader may realistically require a six- to eight-week scheme of work to be able to effectively manage the reading and gain the most impact from the opportunities it presents. Poetry or specific work on developing writing or project-based learning can be much more of a moveable feast: if we are using a collection of poems we have curated, they can be supplemented or reduced to fit into four weeks or five.

In one of my departments, a colleague worked with a nurture group who really needed a little more time on a class reader than the remainder of the year group. This was fine. My colleague spent an extra two weeks on the novel, then covered fewer poems in less time, but was still able to embed the Key Progress Indicators (KPIs) for those students. So, the time factor for each unit of work is the first decision to make to conceptualise the big picture for your scheme of work. A big picture starting point can be done collaboratively in department meetings or CPD time if you are revisiting schemes or adding a new scheme to your curriculum.

It might look something on the right, though in reality mine are often scribbled on the back of an envelope at the moment when inspiration strikes me!

Year 7 4 lessons per week	A Midsummer Night's Dream
Week 1	Reading Act 1
	Do some character stuff: who's who?
	Intro theme of love
	Lysander... letter to Aunt
	The Mechanicals
Week 2	Reading Act 2
	Introducing the fairies
	Do some comprehension questions
	Description/fairies
	Costume designs for display
Week 3	Reading Act 3
	The scenes in the forest with the four lovers/questions
	Feelings of the four characters – Helena and Hermia – hot-seating? Group discussion?
	Writing in role
Week 4	Reading Act 4
	More on Titania and Bottom
	Helena and Hermia argument
	Questions to check understanding of plot/development
Week 5	Reading Act 5
	Resolution
	Questions
	Pyramus and Thisbe group drama performances
Week 6	Assessment task
	Theatre group in
	Mask and prop making
	Display

If we are working with a text such as a playscript or a novel that is new to the department, then the first task – at the risk of stating the obvious – is to read it. You cannot complete the above until you – and the rest of the team – have a working knowledge of the text.

I had a wonderful trainee come to do a first placement in my department some years ago. I assigned her a gorgeous Year 7 group who were just about to embark on their class reader. I gave her a copy of the text to read and at first, this was a surprise to her.

Only when I reflected about my trainee's degree specialism - in Language rather than Literature - did I realise this was not in line with her particular experience or skill-set. I had to understand that a colleague with an English Language degree may never have been asked to read a whole novel or a play or a Shakespeare text in its entirety during their undergraduate study and perhaps not since GCSE.

With every department I work with to develop a curriculum, I begin by doing a skills audit: who in your department has a Literature background or an English Language background? Which area of the curriculum are colleagues most and least confident with? Who has an MA in the Victorian novel? Whose particular interest and specialism is drama? Who is a performance poet at the weekend? Believe me, they are out there! And in the creation of fantastic schemes of work, this is where we can capitalise on those skills, interests and specialisms.

Working with the large department I mentioned earlier, we paired up the fourteen teachers in the team according to their specialist interests, qualifications, and skills. And what an amazingly vibrant working atmosphere we created to revamp the entire curriculum. Not only was the team going to have ownership of their curriculum, but each pair was going to work on a unit they felt genuinely invested in because they could share their expertise.

Task

In your next department meeting or CPD session, do a skills audit within your own team. Check in with their degree study and any further degree specialisms. Establish their key areas of interest and expertise. Do you have any colleagues in your team who are non-specialists who might benefit from a subject expert buddy or mentor?

- Allocate each individual team member - or pairs if you are in a larger department - one or two of the schemes of work in your curriculum plan to take responsibility for moving forward.
- If you are replanning from scratch, put those individuals/pairs in charge of creating specific schemes.
- If you have an existing curriculum in place, put your experts in charge of evaluating and updating the schemes which will be most likely to benefit from their expertise.

Establish the Big Picture

When I am writing resources for my publishers, I often infuriate them. Perhaps I am working on a textbook or a resource that requires a collection of texts. And, of course, this means weeks of work for the publishing team applying for copyright and permissions. When I am asked for information in advance on what texts or extracts I require, my infuriating reply is always, 'I have no idea yet'. The reason for this is because I must find the best text or extract to give me enough mileage to meet the objective or present the skill that I want it to. The outcome is the driving force for the text choice and so this is an evolutionary process.

Conversely, when creating a scheme of work for a class reader or a play, the text itself is the driving force and becomes the vehicle for possibility. It is pointless deciding in advance that in Week 3 of your scheme you will be working on language analysis and description, leading to a piece of descriptive writing, for example, if the chapters of the reader with the richest seam of language to be mined will only be reached in Week 4.

Always read or reread the chosen texts first and, as you read, keep a notebook by your side, jotting down the possibilities as you go. What best use can you make of the text in front of you? What are the possibilities for activities within each chapter or act that will allow you to embed core skills, practice and knowledge? Only then can you successfully create a midterm or week-by-week plan, and not before.

When it then comes to planning out what to include in your week-by-week plans, be very realistic. At this point, do a little experiment for me.

So, in mapping out your week-by-week plan, be realistic in how much of the text can feasibly be read in class in a single lesson before activities around that section of text can take place. I always like to include a variety of approaches for reading. Many of my students (and not even just the younger ones) really enjoy the experience of being read aloud to. For some students, this is an experience they may not even have had at home. The very last Year 11 I had the pleasure of teaching *A Christmas Carol* to would routinely come to my Friday lesson, timetabled for last period in the afternoon – the graveyard shift – and be really exhausted.

'Please Miss: will you just read to us. We're so tired.'

'Yeah Miss, just read to us and do your voices.'

Students often love the experience of reading plays aloud and often volunteer for parts. For a class reader, I like to do some reading aloud myself to maintain the pace and model good practice in terms of fluency and intonation; some with willing volunteers and some using audio recordings if these are available to add variety. To get all students reading, however, I like to construct reciprocal reading groups once I've got to know my class. Not all students feel confident or fluent enough to read in front of a whole class but are often much more willing to build their confidence in a small supportive group with friends they feel safe and comfortable with. Setting a specific number of pages to be read around the group with some follow-up discussion questions can allow more time for those that need it. With some classes you can do flipped reading and end the lesson with the reading for next time, giving you the chance to open the next lesson with some recall discussion.

Once you have established what is being read and when, whether that be a playscript or a collection of poems or a novel, you can then look back at the notes you have made and begin shaping those into the possible skills, knowledge and activities you can cover each week. At this point it's useful to create a document, a little like this, which includes the specifics:

Year 7 Modern prose fiction: *The Girl of Ink and Stars*	
Week 1 × 4 lessons Chapters 1–3	Introducing statement sentences
	Modelling of how to support with quotations
	Introducing adjective and simile as key terms
	Creating a map selecting and retrieving information
	Selecting and supporting ideas about characters
	Building vocabulary knowledge
	Introducing simile, metaphor, alliteration
	Descriptive writing task
Week 2 × 4 lessons Chapters 4–7	Recapping on similes
	Introducing inference
	Introducing concept of myth/legend
	Modelling 3-part comprehension method: statement/quotation/inference
	Introducing main themes
	Character collages
	Knowledge about language
	Narrative writing task
Week 3 × 4 lessons Chapters 8–11	Selection of evidence for a character
	Idea of dialogue and description to create a character
	Concept of symbolism
	Issues of gender
	Letter-writing skills
	Creating a simile poem from a soundscape
	Developing inferential reading skills
Week 4 × 4 lessons Chapters 12–16	Developing knowledge of descriptive techniques
	Describing from an image
	Storyboarding and sequence
	Practising comprehension skills
	Practising selection and retrieval via a creative task
	Creating a drama script

Year 7 Modern prose fiction: *The Girl of Ink and Stars*	
Week 5 × 4 lessons	Developing inference in comprehension
Chapters 17–20	Introducing more language knowledge
	Reciprocal reading with expression
	Creating a diagram with details selected from the text
	Introducing theme and theme collages
	Narrative writing task: writing own chapter
Week 6 × 4 lessons	Analysing description
Chapters 21–25	Lupe's story as a role play
	Crafting a poem on the theme of fearlessness
	Reflecting on the selflessness of characters in the novel as a whole
	An introduction to critical evaluation in groups

And for me, it is only at this point that I can begin to shape my learning objectives, lesson objectives, learning outcomes – however we label our lesson plan with our intentions. This is something that perhaps challenges conventional thinking. We are often taught that we must begin with a clear lesson objective or learning outcome and for the individual lesson plan this is so. However, when we are writing a scheme of work and doing 'big picture' planning, I feel it is imperative to begin at the end. Where will our source material take us? What are its possibilities? How can we use it to our best advantage, to develop skills, to embed knowledge, to allow for stimulating writing outcomes, to promote discussion and critical thinking? You will begin to find that this is much less restrictive; that you won't be trying to fit square pegs into round holes; that the opportunity arises for much more creativity and imagination and therefore engagement in the lessons.

You can see in the example below, from one of my own published resources (Heathcote et al. 2020), how this approach has then resulted in an expansive range of objectives which can be achieved in one scheme of work, giving breadth and variety while also embedding core skills and knowledge.

Year 7, Project 2: Child Labour

* Builds contextual understanding for the following GCSE set texts: *A Christmas Carol*, *Great Expectations*, Romantic poetry

Week	Skill focus	Text	Learning objectives
1	Developing comprehension skills with the 19th-century novel	*The Water Babies* (1863) by Charles Kingsley	• To understand some of the key ideas in an extract from *The Water Babies* • To present and support those ideas clearly • To draw inferences from some of the key ideas in an extract from *The Water Babies* • To present those inferences clearly
2	Developing readings of 18th-century poetry	'The Chimney Sweeper', from *Songs of Innocence* (1789) by William Blake	• To understand the key ideas in a poem through exploring structure • To understand the key ideas in a poem through exploring imagery • To develop skills of making inferences and supporting ideas • To show developing understanding of key ideas and the writer's intention
3	Developing creative writing: Planning creative writing from a picture		• To gather ideas from a picture • To understand how to present the thoughts and feelings of a character • To plan a piece of creative writing • To write from a character's perspective or point of view
4	Developing ideas from 19th-century non-fiction	'Transcript of the Examination of Thomas Priestley' (1806)	• To understand the ideas in an extract of 19th-century non-fiction • To present and support those ideas clearly • To begin to comment on the experiences of others in the past
5	Developing connections with modern non-fiction	'Child labour "rampant" in Bangladesh factories' by Michael Safi, *The Guardian*, 7 December 2016	• To understand and make connections between child labour in the 19th century and today • To use developing comprehension skills to understand key ideas in a broadsheet article • To understand key aspects of language in a news article • To think about the effects of language in a non-fiction text
6	Developing persuasive writing skills: Planning a short speech		• To understand more key techniques for persuasion • To plan for an effective speech presenting a point of view • To write and present an effective speech presenting a point of view

We can then use those activities and lesson objectives/learning outcomes to create the Key Progress Indicators for our students' exercise books or files. In the example below, from another of my own resources (Heathcote and Appleton 2022), you can see how these are directly matched to the lesson objectives but in student-friendly language.

Year 9: *Romeo and Juliet*

Lesson focus	Key Skills Indicators *After completing these lessons I can:*	How well do I understand this skill? ☺ ☺ ☹	Comment and reflection
9.1.1 • Act 1 Sc 1 *'Rebellious subjects, enemies to peace'* Date completed:	Select and retrieve key information. Make inferences about character. Write a detailed comprehension response.		
9.1.2 • Act 1 Sc 2 and 3 *'How stands your disposition to be married?'* Date completed:	Work in a group to present a polished reading. Work in a group to present an exploration of the key ideas in a scene.		
9.2.1 • Act 1 Sc 5 *'She doth teach the torches to burn bright!'* Date completed:	Analyse the language and structure of Romeo and Juliet's first meeting. Understand Shakespeare's intentions.		
9.2.2 • Act 1 Sc 5 *'Too early seen unknown, and known too late!'* Date completed:	Create a mask symbolising a key character.		
9.3.1 • Act 2 Sc 2 *'If thou dost love, pronounce it faithfully'* Date completed:	Work in a pair to explore the development of the key characters. Make developed inferences.		
9.3.2 • Act 2 Sc 3 and 5 *'Wisely and slow; they stumble that run fast.'* Date completed:	Annotate an extract exploring thoughts and feelings of the Friar. Work independently to evaluate the actions of the Nurse.		

Effective resourcing

At this point, once the big picture of a scheme of work has been imagined, the creative work can begin. Again, somewhat obtusely, I write my lesson plan last and, more often than not, revisit my lesson objectives. This is because in the evolution of the lesson, whether via creating a slide deck, developing questions or activities for a worksheet, or searching for images to support a writing task, things can still change. Something that worked in theory in my head may not work in practice. Better to discover now that the brilliant extract of language-rich material I discovered in a first read does not have the simile or example of personification I really needed it to have, than when I've written a perfect plan.

Many schools and Trusts have very specific templates for PowerPoints and these can be limiting and frankly annoying for the creative English teachers among us. I think it is always worth a discussion and a negotiation around these – especially where the seeming non-negotiables have been created or curated by someone whose subject specialism is heavily knowledge led or topic based. Once again, one size does not fit all.

I was very interested in an experiment that Alex Quigley undertook and which he outlines in his work *Closing the Vocabulary Gap*, where he shadowed a student for a day to be able to conceptualise the vast range of subject-specific vocabulary students can be exposed to as they move from class to class, subject to subject. I often wonder what a similar experiment would be like if we shadowed a student through a day where every class used a uniform structure, based around a set of identical PowerPoint templates. At what point might we tire of the retrieval task, the vocabulary slide, and the exit ticket? I was the least sporty girl in my year group when I was in secondary school, but I feel even I would be crying out to put my netball skirt on before too long.

'Less is more' is a mantra I always use when I'm creating a lesson (or a presentation for colleagues) around a slide deck. In lessons I have observed, or at times when I have been supplied with 'The Template' from a client, they are often far too busy, crammed with information and boxes and callouts.

Though we obviously need to be mindful of sustainability, budgets, photocopying and waste, lengthy extracts of text and model answers on slides are cognitively overwhelming for students and they are temporal. Those model responses are not going to be retained in a student's own book for revision.

One element that I introduced into my own resources came from the realisation that the source materials on the examination syllabus we followed contained approximately 650 words per extract. In both my classroom, and my published resources for *Reimagine Key Stage 3 English*, I then aimed for extracts of prose to be stepped, in terms of challenge, from 350 words for Year 7 to 450 for Year 8 and 550 for Year 9, building reading stamina and experience in readiness for the extracts they would meet at GCSE. My publishing team adjust the font size accordingly too.

Having model responses on a clear and attractive worksheet means they can become part of an activity. Students can annotate them with you. They can colour code key skills in line with a mark scheme or a set of success criteria and they can be retained and drawn upon in future tasks. They can have lines added underneath for the student to try out the next paragraph on their own or with a partner.

Creating worksheets for activities shifts the focus away from the screen or whiteboard and places the focus on the desk. Students working on a paired task or group task become more self-contained. Time is saved because the tables, grids or quotations to be explored are pre-prepared rather than needing to be copied from the board. The big headache of textbooks for me always used to be the instruction: make a copy of the table below in your notebook. Who has time for the students to do that? It's why photocopiable teacher guides or accompanying downloads are so useful (and I've always tried to include these in the student resources I publish).

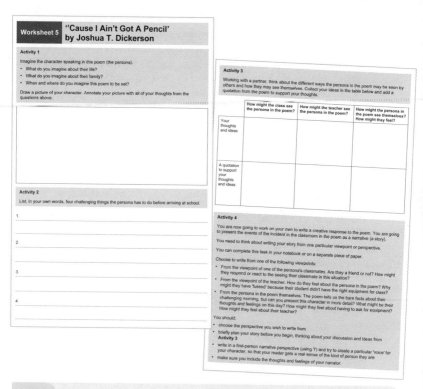

While Barak Rosenshine's 'Principles' (2012) have become common practice in terms of structuring a lesson, at times the complete rigidity with which these extremely effective principles have been applied to lesson planning, and particularly templates for slide decks, can be counterproductive. Good practice surely means including *some* of those principles in each lesson, not *all* of them in exactly the same order every time.

The reviewing of prior learning, for example, may be most effective as a starter activity when we are beginning a week and want to recall key aspects of a plot or key ideas around a poem that we read yesterday if we are going on to explore its language today. At times, though, it may be best placed part-way through a lesson when we recall something that a character has done or said earlier. Only when we realise that Lady Macbeth is troubled by her hands in Act 4 of the play do we realise and need to retrieve the significance of 'A little water clears us of this deed' in Act 2 – quite possibly taught a fortnight earlier – and can provide an 'aha' moment part-way through a lesson.

English is a journey not a destination. We are not 'job done' in three multiple-choice questions. In an article from *Learning From My Mistakes: an English teacher's blog* (2022) by Chris Curtis, this thought is reinforced beautifully:

> ❛Knowledge retrieval isn't that hard to do, but it can become meaningless if it isn't done with thought or understanding. It is so easy to write questions about defining techniques or filling the blanks of quotations, but will it improve their English skills? No. […] If we focus too much on the knowledge, we miss out on the skill and the experience part of the subject. Where is your skill retrieval in the lesson? Where is your experience retrieval in the lesson? Knowledge connects, but it is like a web in our subject. You cannot focus on it alone. There is room for all three parts – knowledge, skills, experience – and English teachers need to ensure there is a balance between all three.
>
> English teachers are the spiders of the knowledge world. We spin our webs all over the place and we wait for some unsuspecting creature to become ensnared in the web. We listen for the vibrations on a thread. We knit connections where are none.❜

A rigidly enforced exit ticket asking a banal question, or for a definition of a word, can be meaningless and contrived compared with having five more minutes to complete a longer written response, or to conduct some proofreading or peer evaluation.

Good practitioners realise the need to include some teacher-talk in their lesson with plenty of active learning and doing, with variety gained from paired or group work and time to consolidate individual skills. A flashing badge on a slide indicating whether this is an 'I do', 'We do' or 'You do' task is a distraction, adding to cognitive load, and could simply be replaced by a clear instruction. Are those badges in existence to benefit the student or are they there as reminders to the teacher because they do not have a plan of their own which they have ownership of?

When picking up the rewriting of a scheme of work for my clients recently, one thing I noticed was that the scheme only consisted of PowerPoints. There were no worksheets, and no lesson plans separate from the slide deck. Even more worrying was that the slide deck contained no notes for colleagues and no timings. If you really want to achieve consistency, then each slide for a lesson must include clarity to enable meaningful delivery. This is especially important where you have less experienced colleagues or trainees. Imagine a different scenario where you were suddenly asked to present a slide deck you hadn't written to a roomful of colleagues at a conference with no notes and no idea of timings for breakouts or activities.

I would always advise that when you are constructing a new scheme of work, the creation of detailed lesson plans is time well spent. They can accompany your slide deck, and each element of the plan can also be added to the deck as notes. The written plan ensures that the whole team have clarity in terms of timing and instruction which will create consistency across the delivery. If you have a newly qualified colleague in your team, a non-specialist who has been brought in to help, or a supply colleague, you are giving them all the help they need to enable them to deliver a high-quality lesson.

Task

Read the lesson plan and selected example slides on the following pages and evaluate how the depth and detail here could help to enable the delivery of a high-quality lesson. Make some notes in response to the following questions:

- How might plans like this assist colleagues who are non-specialists and help to develop subject-knowledge confidence?
- How could using the expertise of your team, gleaned from your skills audit, facilitate the creation of similar detailed plans that would benefit teaching and learning outcomes?

Teaching focus	
A Christmas Carol Stave 3: Lesson 4	
Learning objective(s)	
To understand how Dickens uses language to create a change in the tone of the novel at this point.	
To consider the social and moral contextual message behind the Ghost's visit and begin to understand Dickens' intentions in writing the novel.	
Learning outcome(s)	
Completing a grid exploring the language choices of a key extract.	
Evaluating the use of dialogue to create tone in short-answer questions.	
Contributing valid ideas to a final discussion on the contextual ideas and Dickens' message/intentions.	

Plan to achieve the learning outcomes. Remember:	Starter: [10 minutes]
• I do • We do • You do • Model • Question • Scaffold	**On arrival: (3–4 mins)** Students should complete the short recall activity, reflecting on what they have learned so far about the Cratchit family.
	Objectives shared with student(s) (1 min)
	Big picture (5 mins)
	Introduce the idea of 'tone' and what it means using slide 4. Play students the audio extract from 11.28 to the end (approx 4 minutes). Ask them to jot down their responses to the final bullet point as they listen. Take brief ideas and responses from the whole group as to their suggestions.
	Main learning: [30 minutes]
	Section 1: (15 mins)
	Distribute the worksheet and allow students to work in pairs or small groups to complete the exploration of these key language changes. (slide 5) Students may need support with remembering key terms such as adjectives, verbs, modal verbs and mirroring. With a more able group you might introduce the term 'anaphoric reference' for the final example. Take some feedback and suggestions from various pairs/groups.
	Section 2: (15 mins)
	Allow the same pairs/groups a little more time to explore the dialogue specified on slide 6. Ask students to note down their thoughts and again take feedback and suggestions. Ensure that students understand the contrast between Bob's generous spirit compared with his employer. Mrs Cratchit seems angry on Bob's behalf that he is treated so badly by Scrooge. Ensure that students realise that Scrooge is witnessing this and can see how the others view him.

Teaching focus	
A Christmas Carol Stave 3: Lesson 4	
Learning objective(s)	
Plan to achieve the learning outcomes. **Remember:** • **I do** • **We do** • **You do** • **Model** • **Question** • **Scaffold**	**Consolidation of learning: [15 minutes]**
	Consolidation task: (10 mins)
	Display slide 7. A more difficult section here to guide students through. The tone changes and becomes serious and almost religious; the Ghost's words like a sermon to be learned from. Ensure that students realise that the Ghost is saying the future lives of children like Tiny Tim lie in the hands of the wealthy and those with influence in society to make social change. You may need to define 'penitence'. Ensure that students also see how the Ghost throws Scrooge's earlier words back at him, and it is this that triggers his shame. Use the Ghost's rhetorical question to link to a modern-day context and ask for student suggestions as to whether this is still valid today.
	Plenary: (5 mins)
	Display slide 8 and take a moment with students to explore the moral implications today of having people in society who are desperate and in need of help, such as those seeking asylum or those who need help to feed their families. Whose role is it to help? Look at the Ghost's moral message for Scrooge and Dickens' message to those in positions of privilege in the past, and link to those who are in a position of privilege today.
Literacy and numeracy focus/ support	**Key vocabulary:**
	intentions; contextual; moral; social; modal verb; mirroring; anaphoric; reference; penitence
	Use of tables
Homework task/ Flipped learning task	**Next lesson**
	Ensure that students realise the next section is longer, so prereading is required.
	Homework task (3 min)
	Set up the class for prereading from 'By this time it was getting dark . . .' to 'he left his blessing, and taught Scrooge his precepts.' Ask students to make a list, as they read, of all the different locations the ghost takes Scrooge to.
Evaluation notes on progress	

Exploring the change in tone through dialogue

Dialogue is an important feature of narrative. It allows the reader to 'hear' characters directly and make judgements on them. Look at the part of the scene where Bob Cratchit toasts Scrooge from ' *"Mr Scrooge!" said Bob'* to ' *I have no doubt."'* How does Dickens use dialogue to show us:

a) Mrs Cratchit's feelings. What do you think they are?

b) the different temperaments of Bob and his wife. What do you think they are?

c) the relationship between Bob and his wife. How does the section end or resolve itself?

Slide 6

Consolidation

- What is different about the tone of the Ghost's speech here?
- What moral message is the Ghost giving to Scrooge?
- What is Dickens' wider intention contextually?
- Is there still a message for us today?

"If these shadows remain unaltered by the Future, none other of my race," returned the Ghost, "will find him here. What then? If he be like to die, he had better do it, and decrease the surplus population."

Scrooge hung his head to hear his own words quoted by the Spirit, and was overcome with penitence and grief.

"Man," said the Ghost, "if man you be in heart, not adamant, forbear that wicked cant until you have discovered What the surplus is, and Where it is. Will you decide what men shall live, what men shall die? It may be, that in the sight of Heaven, you are more worthless and less fit to live than millions like this poor man's child.

Slide 7

Consolidation

'Are there no prisons?

'Are there no workhouses?'

Slide 8

Reflection

Take some time to reflect on the quality of materials in your schemes of work.

- Consider the content and construction of slide decks. Would they benefit from being pared down and decluttered? Have they been constructed with clear notes and timings linked to a lesson plan?

- How will the content of those slides be retained by students? Are they linked seamlessly to activities completed in their exercise books or on worksheets?

- Are worksheets clear for all students, attractive and engaging, with clear fonts and clarifying instructions?

- Are extracts of texts clear and manageable for students to read, with space for annotation and activity where needed?

- How are worksheets and extracts retained by students to be useful for future revision and application?

Strategies and takeaways

- **Play to your strengths:** Complete a skills audit across your department and create ownership of your curriculum by applying those strengths to your schemes of work.
- **Big picture before small detail:** Visualise each scheme of work across the weeks and begin by looking for possibility before considering individual lessons, activities and objectives.
- **Quality and clarity:** Ensure that all resources such as slide decks, worksheets and lesson plans are clear, uncluttered and precise to aid high-quality teaching and reduce cognitive load for students.

Chapter 5: Meaningful Methods

Make your methods match your mark scheme

I was very privileged to spend thirteen years of my teaching career in a sixth form college which served, at the time, one of the most deprived areas of Manchester. Students came to this college from a large number of secondary schools across the city, and we had a high proportion of students who needed to resit GCSE English Language and/or GCSE Maths before they were able to progress beyond sixth form. Progression and opportunity were very much part of the mission of the college and so securing improved grades at GCSE was crucial for many students.

It was interesting for me to work with so many students resitting GCSE. During those thirteen years in college, I also served as an Assistant Principal and then Principal Examiner for GCSE English Language, so the one thing I knew inside out was the GCSE mark scheme, how it operated, what it meant and what was needed to hit it. I also saw many thousands of responses over the years. Given that English Language GCSE in its previous incarnations had a Foundation tier – for which I was Principal – I also recognised how many candidates taking the new 9–1 specification might struggle to reach crucial grade milestones. Those milestones would be the key to their progression.

I would always begin the academic year by doing a little research with my new GCSE students. I knew, of course, the grades they had come in with but what was it that had stood in the way of them achieving more highly in the first place? I did the obvious thing and asked them. Students can be remarkably honest with you when they feel safe to do so. In Lesson 1 I gave every student a slip of paper, asked for no names and then, with no nonsense, asked them why they thought they had got the grade they had. Had they missed a lot of lessons? Had they had loads of supply teachers? Did they mess about in class and make a right old nuisance of themselves with their mates? Did they run out of time in the exam? Did they miss loads out in the exam, and if so, why? Did they just not know where to start?

I would keep those slips of paper in my filing cabinet and on the last lesson before their exam I would get them out and read out their anonymous confessions, concerns and worries, and over coffees and cakes we'd talk about how we'd addressed them and how they were going to smash it this time round.

In my initial research time with students, one thing became really apparent time and time again. Students had no real idea what they were being assessed against. They didn't really understand what assessment objectives were and how those related to the mark scheme which was assessing them.

They also had no idea about the mark scheme – many had never seen one – and so they didn't understand which precise skills and aspects of English Language knowledge they were being asked to show in each question.

In my resit classes, I had students from a wide range of secondary schools and therefore the opportunity to view the educational landscape of the city in microcosm. Every student came to GCSE with an armoury of acronyms and different methods that had clearly not served them well. For years and years – right back to the beginning of my career and I suspect beyond that – we were always advised to tell students to use PEE/PEA in their answers (in other words, to use Point-Evidence-Explanation/Analysis). It's a method designed to raise a smile in bored teenagers and get them to write comprehension answers. I'll just repeat that bit and leave it hanging there for a moment: comprehension answers...

What I realised as I worked with resit students was that they simply didn't understand what was meant by this at all. They'd been told it a million times, but they didn't know exactly what was required of them. What exactly was this 'point' they were meant to be making? What constituted 'evidence'? If teachers and examiners wanted a supporting quotation from a text, why did they not just ask for one? And when it came to 'explanation': what were they to explain? The meaning of the words in the quotation or the question or the point or maybe not the meaning at all, but what was implied or suggested to show their actual level of understanding?

Where this became even trickier was when questions asked for a more analytical approach and, of course, GCSE English Language and Literature doesn't just test comprehension skill. When you are dealing with the analysis of language and structure, for example, and requiring a comment on the effect of those choices, when you are dealing with how a writer has crafted a text, then you don't want them to make a 'point' at all. You want students to be able to identify an aspect of language and/or structure through the shorthand that is subject terminology and show their knowledge by giving a precise example of it, not a lengthy quotation which demonstrates no specific knowledge at all.

Once they have done that, you want them to be able to comment on the effect of that choice – again, not what it means. Effect is inextricably linked to 'affect'. How am I affected by this choice made by the writer? How am I affected by this beautiful metaphor? This sequence of visceral adjectives? This collection of violent and dramatic verbs? This stunning use of pathetic fallacy? This dramatic cliff-hanger? And we are affected by them, aren't we? We, as readers, can experience a physical and emotional response to the choices a writer makes. It's why we remember and fall in love with our own favourite writers. Even as I sit here and type, I remember the frisson I felt when I encountered some of Jeanette Winterson's metaphors at various points in my life.

I remember the way Jackie Kay structured a particular short story so that the ending made me want to write to her and say, 'Why? Why did you just leave them there? Please tell me they are okay'.

I remember turning over the last page of a Stella Duffy novel and just gasping at a final realisation. Someone moved away from me on a train recently because I snorted so loudly when I laughed at Grace Dent's memoir of her Northern upbringing, so *affected* was I at how reminiscent it was of my own.

So, we are talking about two totally different things when we are dealing with:

- comprehension skill – currently labelled AO1 across all the GCSE specifications and
- linguistic, structural and grammatical analysis – currently labelled AO2.

That raises the question: what has PEE or PEA got to do with either of those things? Or PETALs, PEAZLs and Woozles? This realisation led to me making some sweeping changes to the way I prepared my own students for resitting GCSE about a decade ago. I focused on two key questions to enable students to distinguish clearly between these two separate skills and assessment objectives:

For AO1 comprehension: *what* do we learn; *what* do we understand?

This allowed me to address retrieval on its simplest level and inference on a higher tariff level.

For AO2 analysis: *how* does the writer show us; *how* do we respond?

This allowed me to upskill students to confidently identify key aspects of language and structure as a starting point and then develop commenting on effect as a higher-order skill.

The higher-tariff skills of AO3 and AO4 for English Language I presented as 'The What–How Combos' where both AO1 and AO2 skills are required to be shown in a combination and developed. This was something I took further to help students structure their GCSE Literature responses using those same methods and that same vocabulary once I went back into secondary school teaching. In this way, the Literature essay became an extension of the work they had previously done on critical evaluation as it followed the same principles.

For me, and most importantly for the students, there was a clear and logical structure through the skills and knowledge required at GCSE for both Language and Literature, based on these questions:

Can I retrieve information from a text?

Can I use comprehension skill to show my knowledge about possible meanings in a text?

Can I do this with more than one text?

Can I do some forensic work and examine the language in a text?

Can I do some forensic work and examine the structure of a text?

Can I piece those skills together and do them at the same time?

Can I piece those skills together and do them with more than one text?

Can I piece those skills together and apply them to a whole poem, novel, or play, also considering my knowledge of its context and the possible intentions of its writer?

It was this approach that I was then lucky enough to be able to publish in my textbooks. First, in my thirty-week GCSE Resit course for post-16 students, which was then reprinted to provide a complete GCSE course for use in secondary schools.

I shared this approach at a conference where I was speaking in 2017 as we evaluated the first round of the revised specification examinations and unpacked some of the questions on a particular GCSE specification. I showed delegates how we could help students much more if we made our methods *directly* match the mark schemes so that we eliminated as many misconceptions for students as possible and so there could be real clarity for students in terms of what was required of them.

A really brilliant colleague and superb English specialist came to me afterwards and said: 'I've been teaching all these years. I cannot believe I have never thought of that. Make the method match the mark scheme. It's so simple and it makes so much sense.'

It is so simple. But I would never have thought of it either had it not been for Gilbert and Mohamed and Khadijah and Sam and Lisa and Claire and Hakim and Laila and the many other GCSE resitters who were happy to tell me why they – in their own words – had 'failed' first time around.

Knowing what's expected

One of the main things I aim to challenge in my consultancy work is the idea that English, as a subject, is full of abstracts. In this context, the old adage 'there is no right or wrong answer' could not be more unhelpful, and it's one of the most damaging phrases I have heard English teachers say. Now, of course, we know what we mean by that. We mean that it is possible to interpret things differently. That our reader response is very different dependent on our experiences, our lives, our cultures, our faiths, our upbringing. The passage that provoked one woman's snort of laughter on a train might barely raise a smile if you hadn't grown up in a small town in the north of England in the 1970s. But look at that phrase 'there is no right or wrong answer' from a student's perspective. Is it really reassuring them to have a go or is it leaving them floundering, without knowing where to begin?

Here, clarity of method is essential. It provides the pegs for students to hang their hats on. It gives every student the opportunity to hit the criteria on the mark scheme to some degree. And it's also important for students to have access to and to understand mark schemes. After all, this is what their final outcomes will be judged against.

Mark schemes can look confusing for students. They are often lengthy, and the numbers and levels and bands do not reveal the all-important grades which students are interested in. Indeed, some of the students I have worked with recently are even confused by the papers themselves. It's hard for students to conceptualise and retain all the information for up to four GCSE papers in English Language and English Literature when they are also trying to retain the information for Maths, Science and all of their optional subjects.

One of the things I found most useful when I was delivering training to teachers about GCSE was the map of the learning journey provided in the training materials. This was a simple diagram which colour-coded the questions through the AQA examination papers by assessment objective and provided the question stem for each.

Here is the example for AQA GCSE English Language (AQA 2017):

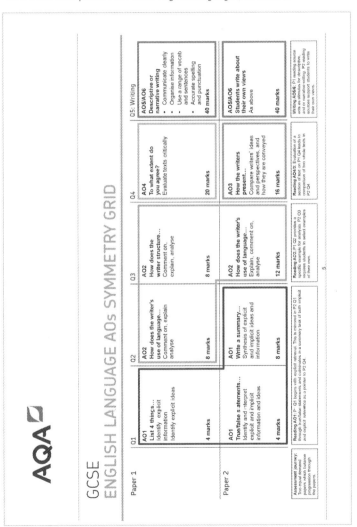

A simple diagram like this, for whichever specification you are studying, can be a really useful thing to stick inside exercise books on Day 1 of your GCSE courses, and it can also be replicated for Literature. It provides a constant reminder of the papers and the required skills for each.

I then translated this diagram for my own students into a wall display: a GCSE learning wall which showed the journey of the questions, the questions stems, our methods to match the mark scheme and some key vocabulary. If you are lucky enough to be able to teach English in specific rooms, displays like this can be utilised in every lesson as a key reminder of where you are up to, which question you are working on, how many marks it is worth and which method to use. This reinforces the key information for students constantly until it becomes second nature. This was probably the lowest-budget resource I ever had – and the thing I used most in the classroom and kept referring back to. Again, this can be replicated for Literature.

From this, with each question I taught at GCSE, I would always provide a simplified mark scheme and begin each set of lessons by unpacking the question and the mark scheme itself. What exactly is being tested? What are we looking for? The students' method would therefore be an evolution of that process. Here, by a simplified mark scheme, I mean the grids or tables the exam board use themselves for their examiners but without the additional information or marking guidance that is provided for the primary audience of the mark scheme: the examiner.

Where students are in sets and aiming for particular target grades, consider just using part or parts of these simplified schemes. For a student who is just beginning their journey in English, for a student who needs additional help with English; for a student who is desperately working hard to achieve a Grade 4 pass in English, seeing a mark scheme looming over them with a skyscraper of skills can be massively demotivating. However, seeing the half of the mark scheme they realistically need to hit, with clear guidance and modelling of how to achieve this, can make the journey seem much more achievable. Even using just one grid at a time can help to move students gradually up the ladder of skills and give them a sense of progress. Once they can achieve the required skills in Level/Band 1 of whichever specification you teach, then give them Level 2, and so on.

Then, rather than the acronym – which may cause misconceptions for many of your students – be clear about what it is you *actually* want them to do.

Reflection

Look at the PowerPoint slide below which gives a clear instruction to enable students to hit the required skills in this AQA mark scheme for an AO2 language analysis task.

Reflect on:

- How does the slide achieve this?
- How might this also assist with peer- and self-assessment?

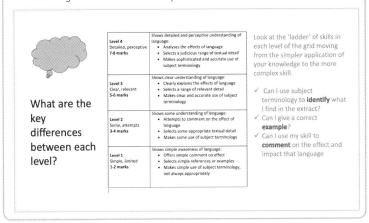

With my own students, and subsequently in my published resources and textbooks, I was able to develop two clear sets of instructions for students that gave them a method to answer any question.

For AO1 tasks beyond simple retrieval: what do we learn; what do we understand?

Always:

- make a clear statement to address the focus of the question.
- support that statement with a quotation from the text.
- make an inference to show what you understand; what is implied; what is suggested; what the possibilities are.

For AO2: how does the writer show us; how do we respond?

Always:

- identify a feature of language or structure and give it its correct name
- make sure you give a precise example or examples of it
- comment on the effect of it on you: what does it make you think of/feel/ imagine: how does it make you respond?

For higher-tariff comparative or critical evaluation questions, I was able to model for students how combining these same methods enabled them to answer those questions effectively and efficiently while not giving them any more approaches to memorise or have to worry about.

Where writing is concerned, mark schemes can often be quite unwieldy. There is, no doubt, a lot to pack in and most mark schemes need to address both the content of writing and the technical skills of candidates. The reminders we give, time and time again, to 'check your work through' can often feel redundant without precise guidance and instruction. As an aside, I am a big fan of 'read aloud' for writing tasks. Pairing students up with a proofing partner they feel comfortable reading their work aloud to, is a great way for them to mutually identify slips in grammar, missed out words and endless sentences.

Using student-friendly checklists, based on the criteria in the mark schemes from your chosen specification, can help students to conceptualise the kinds of things to look for in their own work. If used in conjunction with every writing practice task, over time this skill becomes second nature, and something they can apply in an exam, where the checklist is not available. These checklists can be tailored to suit the ability level of the Key Stage 3 year group in line with the Key Progress Indicators (see Chapter 2) or with the GCSE set in line with the parameters of the mark scheme at each level.

Here's an example of a writing checklist for students:

Organisation

Have I used paragraphs properly to mark the topic shifts in my writing?

Does my work have a clear opening/introduction and a clear sense of an ending?

Have I included any interesting structural features to help shape my writing?

Content

Is my piece of writing clear to read from beginning to end?

Have I used ideas and details to make my piece of writing interesting?

Am I really sure about the purpose and have I stuck to it all the way through?

Have I used the right kinds of language features for this purpose?

Have I remembered who I am writing for and made it sound right for them?

Have I used my strongest, most imaginative vocabulary?

Accuracy

Have I written in Standard English?

Have I used lots of different types of sentences to make the writing more interesting?

Have I remembered to punctuate my sentences?

Have I checked that I've used apostrophes correctly?

Are all my basic spellings okay and my tricky words as good as I can get them?

Task

- Visit the mark schemes for the GCSE specifications that you teach for both English Language and English Literature.
- Take screen grabs of the mark scheme grids or tables without the additional information provided for examiners.
- For each question, aim to identify what the key skills are in *each* band or level of the mark scheme. What pattern do you see? Are they in a logical order from lowest-order to highest-order skill, or do they provide a different logical sequence?
- Now, rather than resorting to an acronym, create a set of clear instructions for each question. What would you like to see your students doing on the page to hit those skills?
- Finally, consider how you can simplify those instructions into a bullet-pointed checklist for success so that they are crystal clear for your students.

Now you have a method to directly match your mark schemes for GCSE!

If we think back to where we began our planning in Chapter 1, working back from our Key Stage 4 'anchor points' we can see now how the dots can join up right through the spiral of our curriculum. Once we have clear and defined methods for the GCSE specification we teach, we can begin to use that same vocabulary and those same key instructions across the department consistently and right from Day 1 of Year 7. If we look back at the example KPI grids on pages 29–31 we can now see that gradual building of skills through Key Stage 3 and into Key Stage 4 with clearly defined methods for comprehension and analysis means that our students are on a logical and much simpler journey to success, enabling them to conceptualise and see their own progress.

Task

In your next department meeting or CPD time, look closely at the mark schemes for Writing in your chosen specification and create student-friendly checklists to use for self- and peer- assessment.

Go on to create checklists which would be manageable for each year group to help them build their skills and improve their accuracy.

Strategies and takeaways

- **Make your method match your mark scheme:** Ensure a consistent and clear approach directly linked to the requirements of the mark schemes of your chosen specification right across the department in terms of the methods you give to students.
- **Create simplicity:** Give as much clarity to students as possible about their paper, the questions, the mark schemes and what's required of them. Keep the methods simple too.
- **Begin at the beginning:** Introduce your methods simply throughout Key Stage 3 so they are fully embedded by GCSE study and every student feels secure and confident with them before they have to apply them to GCSE texts.

Chapter 6: Assessment with Impact

To examine or not examine?
That is a big question

There is a skill to creating meaningful assessments and meaningful examination papers. This becomes apparent when one of them fails to work or deliver the outcomes or information we need it to. Having operated as a Principal Examiner and sat through interminable but necessary, and sometimes heated, question paper evaluation meetings where every single comma was debated over for hours on end, I look at examination papers now with a highly critical eye.

The idea of assessing English through final examination only is a recent and, in my view, regressive step. Looking back at how English has been assessed over the past few decades is very illuminating, as Barbara Bleiman's blog post for the English and Media Centre shows us. She concludes that since 2015:

> There has been stagnation, with no major changes. This has solidified the qualification into something that teachers regard as "normal", though recent surveys by EMC and NATE suggest many are very dissatisfied with it.

Her blog leaves us with several interesting questions to debate and reflect on, not least:

> • How much should the curriculum be nationally determined? How much teacher choice and/or student choice should there be?
> • Are the current ways of examining fit for purpose? For example, split short questions on language and structure in Eng Language; essays and paragraphs rather than other forms of critical writing; creative writing as an exam task and a vehicle for assessing literacy; no spoken assessment.

Barbara's historical overview made me reflective in other ways too. As a 15- and 16-year-old in Set 1 in 1983 and 1984, I completed a portfolio of twelve assignments to gain my Grade A In English Language (A* did not exist should you have worries about my underachievement!). I have memories of writing a short story I was very proud of; of producing a campaign leaflet for nuclear disarmament; of creating a beautiful storyboard for 'The Love Song of J Alfred Prufrock', spending hours and hours sketching it and describing every shot in detail, because I was so enraptured by the poem and because in my mind's eye

I had cast the beautiful boy in sixth form I was desperately in love with in the role of young J Alfred. I kept that storyboard for twenty-five years. I wonder if we could say the same for our GCSE papers now? In contrast, my A Level English was assessed quite differently, with a sequence of three 3-hour papers. It seems that our approach to English assessment in the 1980s had much in common with our Eurovision successes: we were still making our mind up.

I mentioned in Chapter 4 how, during my first teaching practice, I was given the freedom to choose two texts which I was familiar with and excited to teach. This was due to one A Level Literature syllabus at the time – the AEB 660 – assessing through 50% coursework and 50% examination: the best of both worlds. It was, in my opinion, a brilliant specification to teach. You had set texts which were assessed via the examination (for set texts read: the usual suspects – Shakespeare and many classic male poets; I always taught the Metaphysicals so we could do the naughty bits of John Donne) and then you could choose your own coursework texts. This meant you could add diversity to your curriculum; you could put your own collections of poetry together; you could choose texts that would engage specific cohorts of students. It meant I could sit in a classroom of all White students in a northern mill town and teach Maya Angelou's *I Know Why the Caged Bird Sings* and Grace Nichols' *The Fat Black Woman's Poems*. If there was going to be a production of *Death of a Salesman* or *The Crucible* or *A Taste of Honey* or *Cat on a Hot Tin Roof* in any of the local or regional theatres, we could capitalise on that. We could teach it and take students to see a production of it. Choice in assessment and a curriculum brings those responsive opportunities.

So why did we see, in reform, death of coursework? The answer, for me, lies mainly in one place: league tables. The ideology of measuring school performance by creating a rank order, pitching schools one against the other with little regard for contextual factors.

Every year, as a Principal Examiner sitting on a panel confirming grade boundaries, we would see hundreds of examples of coursework folders and hundreds of examples of examination papers and would need to meticulously tick or cross charts and use professional judgement to confirm grade boundaries. Grade boundaries which were statistically generated to maintain the glass ceiling, which is the comparable outcome, thereby preventing grade inflation year on year. The only real manoeuvre available was to balance the exam outcome against the coursework outcome. The more that coursework was seen to be leniently rewarded overall, the more the boundary mark had to increase to compensate for it.

We have a much greater understanding now of the examination system thanks to extensive CPD and more transparency, but then many colleagues, many heads of department, and indeed very many senior leaders did not fully understand comparable outcomes. There was widespread discontent from schools who religiously applied the mark schemes, studied the exemplar materials, and moderated their coursework scrupulously that other schools 'down the road' (they were always down the road) were pushing the boundaries of 'tolerance'. But why might that school down the road be driven to do that? Lack of experience perhaps. Lack of training and CPD perhaps. Fear of being placed last in local league tables – more likely. Fear of being placed in special measures with all that follows – also likely. The loss of coursework assessment in English is, for me, the most regrettable collateral damage of this system.

Any meaningful assessment should, in my view, be organic and responsive, in just the same way our teaching should be responsive, to enable candidates to succeed. An assessment in English should be a vehicle for a student – or in a public examination, a candidate – to demonstrate their best skills and I would go so far as to question whether an examination paper is really the best vehicle for that.

Creating meaningful assessments

In the course of a student's five-year journey through secondary school, we are likely to have a number of assessment points before they reach the summative assessment of GCSE. When *we* are creating internal assessments for English within our departments, we have to ask ourselves some key questions:

- What exactly are we testing or assessing? Are we simply testing knowledge, for example, some key spellings, the parts of speech, key literary terms? Are we testing skills, for example, at the end of a sequence of lessons on persuasive writing or having taught a Shakespeare play at GCSE?
- Why are we testing or assessing? What is it we need to know from the outcomes of this test or assessment? Do we want to identify gaps in knowledge, for example, so we can plan to fill those gaps in future lessons? Do we want to gain a picture of how far our students have come in terms of a particular skill so that we can work out how best to develop it further, for example, in creating engaging and effective narratives?
- How best shall we do that testing or assessment? Through a simple test or quiz? Through the creation of longer-answer questions? Through setting a common assignment? Through a group challenge? Is the answer always an exam paper or have we been conditioned to think so in recent years?
- How will we mark or adjudicate that test or assessment? What will our criteria be? How will we apply the criteria consistently to be fair to every student?
- How will we feed back to our students to benefit them and make that feedback part of meaningful progress?
- What will we do with the outcomes of that testing and assessment?

Reflection

Think about the points in the year at which you test students through Years 7–11.

- What procedures are followed? What do you test at those various points in the year? Does the testing directly correlate with what has been taught in any given period?
- Do all your students know why they are being tested and what they need to demonstrate within the assessment?
- Does the assessment method sufficiently allow for students to show their best skills, for example, in creative writing?
- How do you use the outcomes to inform your future planning and evaluate the success of your curriculum?
- How do you feed back to students so they can see precisely what they need to do to improve? Is sufficient time given to this process?

Recently, I looked at some centrally produced assessment papers that a cluster of schools were using to test pupils at key stage 3. The paper tested reading skills and comprised passages of prose fiction followed by several questions – not so unusual you may think. However, on checking, I noted that the volume of reading on the Year 7 English mid-term assessment was greater than that of a GCSE paper, so that created food for thought. Many departments test students on a half-termly or termly basis and base their assessments on the topic or text that has been taught in that timeframe. This, however, is not always the case. Working with one large trust recently, it came to my attention that Key Stage 3 students were being tested using some centrally produced assessment papers. In terms of consistency; so far so good. The paper tested reading skills and comprised passages of prose fiction followed by several questions – not so unusual, you may think. I asked the Head of Department I was working with what the word count was of the passages. She wasn't sure, so we checked. The volume of reading on the Year 7 English midterm assessment was greater than that of a GCSE paper, so that created food for thought.

Should we not be creating assessments for our students which help them to progress towards their final goals, and see those steps clearly, rather than setting them up for failure? In Chapter 4 I mentioned that the examination specification I chose in my last teaching post used extracts of texts that were approximately 650 words in length and that in the projects I created for *Reimagine Key Stage 3 English*, I scaled back the reading demand from there: 350 words in Year 7, 450 in Year 8, 550 in Year 9. This could be a useful rule of thumb when building reading assessments. Look at the demand of your GCSE specifications and then scale back accordingly.

If we think back to our spiral from Chapters 1 and 2, we can create a logical assessment journey for our students in the same way we created a learning journey. We also have a road map for what should be assessed through our Key Performance Indicators. If they provide the checklist for our students as to what they have been working on that term or half term, matched to the scheme of work, then they also surely provide the blueprint for what we should assess them on.

Task

Look at the table below. Even without specific texts in place at Key Stage 3, what assessment opportunities can you see along the horizontal time frames of each academic year?

How could this lead to a more logical assessment journey for students through the vertical spiral? Use the final row of the grid to jot down your ideas.

	Autumn 1	Autumn 2	Spring 1	Spring 2	Summer 1	Summer 2
Year 7	Work of Prose Fiction/class reader Narrative Writing	Poetry Descriptive Writing	Drama text	19th Century project	Shakespeare text	
Year 8	Work of Prose Fiction/class reader Narrative Writing	Poetry Descriptive Writing	Drama text	19th Century project	Shakespeare text	
Year 9	Work of Prose Fiction/class reader Narrative Writing	Poetry Descriptive Writing	Drama text	19th Century project	Shakespeare text	
Year 10	20th and 21st Century Fiction AQA GCSE English Language Paper 1 Skills and Knowledge Narrative writing	Poetry anthology: Power and Conflict AQA GCSE English Literature Paper 2 Skills and Knowledge Descriptive writing	Drama *An Inspector Calls* AQA GCSE English Literature Paper 2 Skills and Knowledge	19th Century and Modern Non-fiction AQA GCSE English Language Paper 2 Skills and Knowledge	Shakespeare *Macbeth* AQA GCSE English Literature Paper 1 Skills and Knowledge End of Year 10 Assessments Spoken Language Assessment	
Year 11	Unseen Poetry x 4 weeks 19th century Novel x 8 weeks *A Christmas Carol* AQA GCSE English Literature Papers 1 and 2 Skills and Knowledge Mock examinations		Revision AQA Paper 1 GCSE English Language AQA Paper 2 GCSE English Literature	Revision AQA Paper 2 GCSE English Language AQA Paper 1 GCSE English Literature Final mocks	Revision and start of final exam period Closing the final gaps	Final exam period
Assessment opportunities in…						

It seems obvious that at the end of Autumn 1, we might assess our students on reading comprehension and narrative writing if these skills have been (surely) included in our scheme of work for class readers in Years 7–9. Thinking back to our KPIs, we may have introduced some language analysis in Year 8. We may have introduced first steps into critical evaluation in Year 9. We might set our comprehension and analysis tasks here using passages from our chosen class reader that have not been utilised in class. Our writing tasks might focus on the themes or ideas or a line from those texts as a title. This would lead us seamlessly into our chosen specification's paper based on unseen prose fiction in Year 10 and our more complex nineteenth-century novel in Year 11. It creates a stepped approach from the familiar to the unseen.

In Autumn 2 we might test some inferential reading through the poetry and some key figurative language terms, then perhaps over the years, introduce more questions of an analytical nature which explore the poet's choices in terms of language and structure. By Year 9 we might be able to test students' ability to compare poems in a manageable way as a stepping-stone into the GCSE skills.

If we were creating assessments for Shakespeare, we might lead them gently towards GCSE assessment by using an extract of the play they had studied every year from Year 7. In Year 7 we might set a series of short-answer or multiple-choice questions – maybe followed by a fun writing task where they could get into character or respond creatively to an aspect of plot.

In Year 8 we might set a sequence of slightly longer-answer inferential reading tasks, perhaps followed by some selected phrases or examples of methods from Shakespeare to identify and comment on. In Year 9 we might set a more combined comprehension and analytical task – a 'what + how' combo – purely based on the extract. Thereby, we have created a spiral of skills leading them to the GCSE Literature 'part to whole'-style questions. Now, when we look at the outcomes of student assessments, we can see progress not just horizontally through the year groups, but vertically too.

This approach means we can see who is still struggling with particular skills from Year 7 to Year 8 and into Year 9, which also enables more effective and targeted intervention to be put in place.

Creating consistency in assessment

One of the biggest misconceptions I come across when working with departments that are marking mock exam papers and Key Stage 3 assessments is understanding the difference between moderating and standardising. Many departments routinely set test papers and complete several rounds of mock examinations and tell me they achieve consistency by moderating. Nonsense. 'What?!' I hear the shrieks from here.

Moderation happens after marking has taken place. In a department, you may have three, four, even ten or fifteen people marking. Revisiting papers after they have been marked and attempting to achieve consistency is both time-consuming and ineffective. Is it really efficient to look back at marking and try and encourage people to change marks they are convinced are right in the first place?

Moderation is what we do with coursework, when, feasibly, every teacher might have taught a separate text or set a different task. It's about balancing out a fair standard across lots of different responses and approaches. When every student sits the same paper, we should *not* be moderating. We should be standardising.

As a Principal Examiner, when numbers on my GCSE paper were at their highest, I would spend three days with my Assistant Principals selecting and creating a set of five beautifully annotated standardising scripts. They were crucial. Alongside the mark scheme, they were our primary tools for creating consistency across over 700 examiners, who we were desperately trying to ensure marked within one mark of the set standard on each question. The number of marks between grade boundaries can often be very narrow, so markers veering beyond the accepted levels of tolerance could ruin the life chances of the individual 16-year-old whose answers they were marking. A little dramatic perhaps but... exam results are a serious business, aren't they?

Rather than trying to close the gate after the horse has bolted, *always* set a standard before you begin marking any batch of papers. Set aside a department meeting or your CPD time and put the entire cohorts' papers on the table in front of you. Now, use your department knowledge. Which students are likely to have done extremely well? Which are in the middle and which are your lower and lowest achievers at this point? Build yourselves a set of standardising materials. This could be done as whole papers at Key Stage 3, but question-by-question at GCSE to really show good practice. At the very least, aim for a set of materials which shows top, middle, and lower levels of achievement. For GCSE, aim to have exemplars from each band or level of your specification's mark scheme.

When you've chosen your exemplars, photocopy them for the whole team and then sit down and mark them collaboratively. You will know within 20 minutes who is the most lenient marker in your team and who is the most severe. I promise you.

The idea here is that in creating these materials you come to agreement, before anyone has touched their marking, as to what is and isn't acceptable. You have agreed on what you want to see for something to be all Level 3 or all Band 2. And you must come to a consensus. The person who is severe will need to temper their desire to circle every spelling error at the expense of seeing the good attempts at using vocabulary. The person who is lenient will have to stop saying 'but I can see what he's trying to say' when a student's response is patently not clear. You need everyone on the same page before you allow a red or green or purple pen anywhere *near* a single exam paper.

The standard is set, and everyone must stick to it.

Now, this is the bit where you need to get the cakes out as a department or Key Stage leader. No one should be leaving the building with their own class's papers. (I hear more shrieks. It's like Banquo's Ghost has moved in for this chapter. I feel a lot of gory locks being shaken at me.)

Ever wondered about the other reason why coursework marks tended towards the lenient? One remarkable thing that I noticed in the privileged position I held was that, when teachers marked their own students' coursework, they were generous souls. Of course, we were! We'd probably spent a minimum of two years with our students; sometimes we had known them right from when they were sweet Year 7s. We had seen lots of their work. We always knew what they were trying to say even when they weren't quite saying it. We saw the very best in them and we rewarded it. Sometimes by a bit too much.

But I can tell you, hand on heart, that when teachers become examiners in a public examination, a strange metamorphosis happens. Mary Poppins becomes Cruella de Vil. It was rare to find an examiner who was lenient. The natural tendency was for severity. I often had real trouble encouraging examiners to use the full range of marks on a mark scheme. It was why the standardising material was so crucial.

I know the argument. 'But I want to mark my own papers. I want to see how my own students have done.' That way inconsistency lies. Look at the papers when you get them back. For now, let them go. Spread the love.

Consider the improved consistency you will get across your team if each team member takes responsibility for a single question. Mark them in batches of perhaps 30 at a time and then pass them on, so no one is waiting too long for the marker who needs more time on their designated question. In this way, you will develop specialists within your team who have an overview of the achievement of the whole cohort in terms of specific AOs, questions, or particular set texts. They will be able to report back much more consistently and knowledgably on what the picture looks like across the whole cohort so you can plan much more effectively, as a team, the ways to address gaps in knowledge and skills. In this case, if one marker is slightly severe then they have been slightly severe on every student, not just thirty of them. If another marker has been slightly lenient, they have been lenient on everyone's students and not just their own class.

Reflection

- How do you ensure consistency of assessment across your department or team at the moment?

- What are the pros and cons of the system you use?

- How would setting a standard improve consistency and quality of marking in your team?

- What would be the benefit of developing 'question' or 'set text' specialists across your team?

Wave goodbye to the tick

Now, while I'm probably not winning friends but hopefully influencing good practice, I'm going to share with you one of my absolute pet hates in terms of assessment in English. It's the tick. The humble tick. That flick of the red pen popping up in books and on scripts since time immemorial.

When the move was first made to online marking – and trialled on my paper – I came up with a fiendish plan. I banned the tick from every question except the simple retrieval task. I know. Scandalous. Why would I have done such a thing with this beautiful symbol and cornerstone of marking? Simple. It told me nothing in relation to the mark an examiner had given.

When examiners were ticking, the tick did not show me any justification for the mark they had arrived at. Which skill were they rewarding out of all the bullet points in the mark scheme? The tick didn't even communicate to me which level they were placing candidates in, let alone the precise skill.

Instead, I introduced a marking code and a set of abbreviated annotations. Rather than just dragging and dropping a random tick, examiners could drag and drop a specific annotation – which showed their team leader exactly what they were rewarding and flagged up immediately if they had any misconceptions about the mark scheme or why they were deviating from the agreed standard. It helped team leaders to coach their examiners to become better and more accurate markers.

This got me thinking about my marking in class and led me to change the way I marked and annotated here. Now, as well as making my methods match the mark scheme, I also made my marking match the methods which matched the mark scheme. That's a lot of matching, but bear with me.

When I marked students' work at GCSE, I used a code which directly correlated with the student-friendly mark scheme they had pasted into their books. So, as an example, if they were completing a practice language task and the mark scheme looked something like this for my chosen specification:

Level 3 Clear, relevant **5–6 marks**	Shows clear understanding of language: • Clearly explains the effects of language • Selects a range of relevant detail • Makes clear and accurate use of subject terminology
Level 2 Some, attempts **3–4 marks**	Shows some understanding of language: • Attempts to comment on the effect of language • Selects some appropriate textual detail • Makes some use of subject terminology

the method I gave to students looked a little something like this:

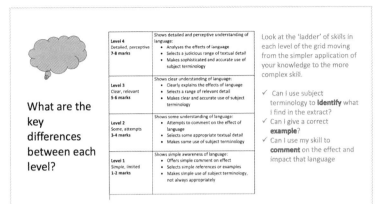

and so the marking code I used was:

LF: identifies a language feature

Ex: gives correct example(s)

SCE: simple, generalised comment on effect for Level 1

Att/eff: attempts a comment on effect for Level 2

C/eff: clear comment on effect for Level 3

Dev/eff: developed or detailed or perceptive effect for Level 4.

I created codes for comprehension AO1, language and structural analysis AO2 and for writing tasks too, all built from the mark schemes. And the benefit of this was twofold. First, when rolled out to my team during rounds of mock and whole-school exams, it massively improved the quality of marking in the department and created consistency. I was also using the codes as a matter of course with classwork when I received an unexpected comment from a student: 'Ooh Miss, I love the way you mark. It's so clear what I've done and what I need to do.' That's when I encouraged it into formative assessment through the exam courses and both Key Stages, creating beneficial consistency, transparency and assessment for progress.

This became a really important way of feeding back to students efficiently. It showed them precisely what they were doing and where; where they were hitting aspects of mark schemes or success criteria, and it helped them to identify what was missing from their responses to help them improve and progress.

Strategies and takeaways

- **Create stepping-stones for achievement:** Use your spiral curriculum to create assessments which test skills and knowledge not just 'horizontally' through one academic year, but which create a vertical sequence of logical assessments through the five-year journey.

- **Join the dots:** Ensure that assessments directly match up with the skills and knowledge you have taught in each term or half term. Give clear instructions to students on test papers and use bullet points to remind them of the methods you want to see.

- **Spread the love:** Ensure consistency of marking mock examinations and Key Stage 3 assessments by setting a standard first, not chasing it. Resist letting the department mark their 'own' classes. Develop a culture of objectivity through establishing question/text/skill specialists.

- **Make marking mean something:** Remember, the tick means nothing in terms of meaningful feedback for progress. Develop a useful code for precision application of mark schemes and clarity of feedback to students.

Chapter 7: Let the Adventure Begin

Finding the soul

English departments and teams are part of the beating heart of any school or college. As I said right at the start of this book, English is far more than a set of data on a spreadsheet, it's far more than Grade 5s and 7s and 9s.

Without the very basics of English, our students will struggle to cope with day-to-day life: the myriad of information life places in front of them and the deluge of admin. Filling in a form or responding to an email or articulating themselves in a job interview will be difficult for some of our students.

But beyond that, the study of English is part and parcel of the development of critical thinkers, enquiring minds, fulfilled souls, lifelong readers and learners. English itself is an enriching experience if taught properly with heart and with soul. You are responsible for that for all of your students. The idea for this book began with the little sheet, shown on the next page, that I gave to my Year 11s when they left school as the pandemic hit, knowing they would not sit their exams and unsure of how they would be assessed instead.

Final Very Very Important Homework

Critically evaluate the following for its:
- artistic merit
- intellectual rigour
- chances of ever being published in an AQA anthology.

A heartbeat ago I walked into this room
And filled you all with buckets of doom
With my new fangled methods and essays to plan
If looks could have killed, I'd be just like Dun .... can.
But now three years later, you are seeing it through
With reminders to take SQI/IEC along with you;
Not just in the exam, but always through life:
Be always *supportive*, your *examples* sound,
Be curious, read widely, keep your feet OFF the ground!
Pay a *VISIT* often to a beautiful poem
Never be afraid to let your imagination ro ... am (poetic licence!)

For you who have wrestled with Banquo's ghost,
And cursed all those witches each day with your toast;
You who have sighed o'er the words of Browning
And let Ozymandias keep you frowning;
You who were outraged at how Birling lied
And shed a small tear, knowing how Eva died;
You who have seen the changed Ebenezer
Have realised Will Shakespeare was such a top geezer.

English is not just about Sevens and Nines
And who can jump hurdles and grade boundary lines.
It's about *loving* words and all they can do -
Scoop them up in your arms; take them with you.
It's about finding meaning in books you can treasure
And oodles of soul food no exam board can measure.
So 'Forward! The Eleven Brigade.'
Put on a brave face.
Our plot ended with a twist,
But you are in a good place.

With love and good luck to you all

Mrs Heathcote

English, as a subject, as a department, needs to be a place where students want to come, are hungry to learn, love what they are doing, are prepared to think hard, think outside of boxes, think beyond PowerPoint slides – and that gives us much to reflect on in terms of our own practice.

In recent years I have often been asked to deliver 'masterclasses' to large groups of students and, having done this a few times, I have started to say no to these requests. Throwing 100 students in a hall with me, a complete stranger, and hoping something will stick does not make a masterclass.

A masterclass – or should I say best class given my early concerns about 'mastery' – is the Friday afternoon when you let your Year 11s keep their coats on in a classroom where the heating has gone on the blink again, shut the door and read them *A Christmas Carol* 'in all your voices'. It is when someone in a tricky Year 9 set turns round and says: 'Why do these lessons always seem to go so fast Miss?' It is when one of your A-Level students shows up for your revision lesson with their coursework in one hand and their tiny scrap of a three-week-old baby in the other and you teach the class walking round with the baby in your arms, so she can take notes. Those are a few of mine, and they could be yours too. Are you brave enough and, if so, how do you create that warmth, that feedback that you don't ask for, that loyalty?

The learning environment

The first thing I would say is to look at the learning environment and evaluate it. This holds true if you are moving to a new school, taking up a new leadership position or have been in your existing department for a while. Let's not be naïve: the pandemic changed everything. Departments had to be restructured and classrooms reallocated to create safer learning bubbles for staff and students. Students had to remain in specific spaces for their own safety and yours. Now we are (hopefully) through that period we can perhaps reclaim departmental spaces, creating ownership and a warm, welcoming learning environment. Time spent curating this environment is not wasted and, as well as benefitting your students, it will also massively improve the working environment for the English team. No one wants to work in a cluttered, messy tip with the lights off and the blinds drawn and all eyes on the screen from minute one. That's no good for anyone's wellbeing.

I always used to laugh up my sleeve a little at the scramble into action before Open Evening. The administrative staff would be out in the corridors armed with staple guns whacking up displays left, right and centre to create the impression they were this lovely all the time. Then they would stay there for twelve months becoming increasingly faded and ignored until October rolled round again.

Display is so important in the English classroom and particularly displays of student work. Rather than giving yourself the Ofsted/Open Evening panic, aim to plan for display within your actual scheme of work. If you are about to teach a class reader in September, consider preparing a display board in every classroom for that title, so that beautiful examples of student work can be added to it over the weeks or in the final week of study to curate a display with the class themselves. Years 7 and 8 love this and it's an important way to encourage pride and engagement in their work if everyone has the chance to contribute to the display.

I would then advocate changing these and refreshing the backing once a term to prevent work being spoilt and displays beginning to look tatty. Built into your scheme of work, this is not a 'make work' project for you, but instead an opportunity for students to engage. Teaching *Romeo and Juliet* with my Year 9, I set up a homework project to design a mask for the Capulet feast for a character of their choice. Students had to provide a written commentary for their mask, saying why it matched that character's personality, behaviour and language. I provided templates and craft materials for anyone who wanted to take them, or students could make use of their own materials if they were lucky enough to have them. The display they created filled almost an entire wall and was stunning. It did more for the engagement with the play than watching Baz Luhrmann with the blinds shut. The students were invested and had ownership of their learning environment.

In Chapter 6, I shared the idea of creating a cheap and cheerful learning wall for GCSE. A display such as this, if laminated or coated with clear protective covering, can become a permanent fixture and one you can refer students to time after time as part and parcel of your teaching. 'What do we know about Question 4?' 'What are the methods?' 'What is our timing?' 'Which AOs are being tested?' 'Check the wall.' 'What does this have in common with…?' The display becomes a vehicle for constant oral retrieval of key information without the need for yet another retrieval slide.

I know a wonderful Head of English who had to move out of her beautifully welcoming classroom, to enable the creation of an office, into one that was a bit of a mess, with peeling white paint. Told there was no budget to have it repainted, she went in at half term and did a spot of guerrilla decorating. And bookshelf filling. And cosy chair purloining. And pot plant arranging. 'I'm not spending all those hours teaching beautiful Literature in a room like a tip,' she told me. Now, I'm not suggesting you all 'do an Aisha' and give up your holidays to renovate your classroom, but build the time into your plans to bring your English rooms and corridors to life and you will immediately begin to bring your students' investment in the subject to life.

Reflection

Take some time to consider the learning environment in your department. Perhaps you are lucky enough to be in a new building with a budget for beautiful wall stickers and decoration; perhaps you are in an older building with little budget for improvements.

Evaluate the learning environment for your students with fresh eyes:

- Imagine you are a new student walking into those rooms for the first time, or an existing student walking in day after day. Are the rooms warm, tidy, and inviting?

- What is there in the room to encourage students to fall in love with English? How do the bookshelves look? What is on the walls? Is there anything here which will help them to learn and retain key English knowledge? Is there anything which will encourage them to read?

- Is there anything which gives them shared ownership of the space – can they see any of their work of which they may be proud?

Enriching experiences

My youngest daughter has selected her GCSE options ready for Year 10 while I have been working on this book. I told her she could pick absolutely anything she wanted, anything she really liked for GCSE, given that Maths, English and Science were compulsory. I had a little chuckle to myself – and a slight gasp – when I discovered she has made all her other selections based purely on the possible 'trip opportunities'. She's chosen Drama because it means going to the theatre a lot; Art because they will go to galleries a lot: 'I've heard sometimes they go to New York' (bigger gasp); and she's already fleeced me for the deposit for the MFL trip. But these are the things we remember about school, aren't they?

We don't look back fondly on our mock exams, we don't care where we were on the spreadsheet, we don't remember handouts or worksheets or whoop with joy at being hauled in for intervention after school. We remember the times spent with our peers when our teachers organised something a little out of the ordinary: a trip, a school production, a workshop, a competition. Yes, it takes energy, and it takes imagination. But if we don't do it, who will? Who will create those experiences for our students, some of whom have extremely impoverished lives? And frankly, those experiences will do more to impact on your student outcomes than any data drop or extra intervention.

In English, making use of local theatres can be an absolute winner. It's not easy to organise a theatre trip and it can be very expensive. Logistically it can be really difficult, if not impossible, if you have 240 students in a Year 11. However, there are brilliant theatre groups who will come to you and perform full set plays or abridged novels or bring the study of texts to life in other imaginative ways.

Always look up the Education Officer at your local or regional theatre – there will be someone doing that job – and make a personal contact with them. Not only will they have resources, but you can let them know what you are studying and there may be opportunities for collaborative work, workshops and visits from actors and performers.

There are brilliant community arts projects in every town and city. Perhaps task different members of your team to be the drama champion, the poetry champion, and the reading champion (remember those schemes of work experts from Chapter 3?).

What is going on locally? Do you have a young writer's poetry group with brilliant local spoken word artists, such as Young Identity run by the amazing poets Shirley and Nicole May? What is your local bookshop doing? Could they come and share the latest releases with Year 7 and do some reading with them? Do you have a local literary festival where you could tap into visiting authors more cost-effectively while they are in town? Why not make yourself known to the organisers so that you can become part of what is happening locally?

There can be so many opportunities here for your students to have the most amazing enriching experiences. Rather than feeling, 'but we don't have the time', aim to build these opportunities into the curriculum itself, into the schemes of work. Plan the time for them so they are part and parcel of what you deliver as a team, not something extra to find time for when you are exhausted. They will energise and refresh you and your teaching just as much as they will energise and refresh students' learning.

Another good source of enrichment can come from university departments and sixth-form colleges. Who are the tutors on the creative writing BA? Can they come and do a workshop with some of their undergraduates? All students on drama and performing arts courses need audiences. Make some links. Could they come and perform a rehearsed reading of *An Inspector Calls* or an act of *Macbeth* with a workshop? Can they devise something on the themes from *Noughts and Crosses*? If you don't ask...

Several theatre groups offer 'Play in a Day' workshops and performance opportunities for younger students. These are usually cost-effective, and they encourage parents to come and see the performances too, which adds to the engagement.

Look *outwards* into the community from your English classroom. You will feel the benefits and see the impact.

Making a lasting impact

Sometimes, it's hard to see the wood for the trees. And I'm not just talking Birnham. Schools seem to operate at 100 miles per hour and the examination sausage factory just does not help us in what often seems to be a constant race against time.

Students are constantly told that STEM subjects are the way to go and, instead of championing the intellectual rigour of English, the massive contributions that the creative industries make to our economy, the massive impact our subject has on emotional intelligence and critical thinking, we have seemingly allowed ourselves to be repackaged, commodified, reduced to the one size fits all, by those with the biggest voices and the smallest imaginations.

I am hopeful that at least some of the strategies in this book will help you to curate an English curriculum effectively and imaginatively to enable much more fruitful use of time; a logical spiral of gradual skills-building and subject knowledge, where the journey becomes much more seamless and makes perfect sense for your students year on year and which creates time for a broader, richer experience.

Students need to be able to conceptualise and see that journey unfold as much as, if not more than, your senior leaders need to see the data to crunch. And our students deserve a wonderful experience in English, not a reductive one. They will repay you in spades for curating that enriching curriculum and experience for them. The notes and cards and little messages I've received from students and ex-students over the last thirty years have made every hour of time I've put in worthwhile. And they have never stopped making me laugh. I've had much more fun in my own classroom with the students than I've had with many of the grown-ups I've met and worked with over the years. Even when students have left my care and they get in touch, they are still capable of making my day:

Like rn im reading anna karenina   11:33

Which is AMAZING   11:33

Oh my word!   11:33 ✓✓

AND NOW I WISH I COULD READ RUSSIAN BECAUSE LEO TOLSTOY IS A RIGHT GANGSTA   11:33

The job you are doing is vitally important. The subject itself is in your hands and in your care. The love for it, the passion for it, is your responsibility to hand on. Lasting impact comes from a place of love. Only by creating an English curriculum with soul will we be able to believe in it ourselves and share that love.

Reflection

Take a final few minutes to reflect. How much of the subject you love are you really using in your English classroom? How much are you engaging with your own subject and nurturing your passion for it? What three things have you done this week to demonstrate that passion?

Strategies and takeaways

- **Curate a space with soul:** Consider how the learning environment in English might reflect the subject itself and become a place where students want to learn and develop. Consider how this working environment will also aid staff wellbeing.
- **Look for the soul outside:** Look for ways you can provide enriching experiences for students which don't need to be logistically difficult or financially challenging for students or school budgets. Think outside of the box and maximise the opportunities in nearby communities.
- **Feed your own soul:** Never allow your own love for the subject to be diminished, for you are its custodian.

The Ta Dah List

This is definitely not a *To Do* list. Rather it's a list of organisations and websites to help you add sparkle and variety to your English curriculum – and to create those *Ta Dah* moments in your classroom. This list is not exhaustive – there are many more brilliant organisations out there – but it includes those I have found useful in my own classrooms. There is space following the list for you to note down other wonderful organisations in your local area as and when you discover them.

The English Association: https://englishassociation.ac.uk/

NATE: https://www.nate.org.uk/

The Book Trust: https://www.booktrust.org.uk/

The Black Curriculum: https://theblackcurriculum.com/

The Proud Trust: https://www.theproudtrust.org/

Interesting Literature: https://interestingliterature.com/

Young Writers: https://www.youngwriters.co.uk/

Voice 21: https://voice21.org/

Debate Mate: https://debatemate.com/

Young Poet's Network: https://ypn.poetrysociety.org.uk/

Young Identity: https://www.youngidentity.org/

Poetry By Heart: https://poetrybyheart.org.uk/

Foyle Young Poets: https://foyleyoungpoets.org/

Edisodes: https://edisodes.com/

English Theatre Company 'Play In A Day': https://www.englishtheatrecompany.com/

Splats Entertainment (Shakespeare Play In A Day): https://splatsentertainment.com/shakespeare-plays/

The National Theatre: resources and live streamed productions
https://www.nationaltheatre.org.uk/learn-explore/schools/

The RSC: resources and live streamed productions
https://www.rsc.org.uk/learn/schools-and-teachers
https://www.rsc.org.uk/shakespeare-learning-zone/

Shakespeare North Playhouse:
https://shakespearenorthplayhouse.co.uk/

National Youth Theatre
https://www.nyt.org.uk/

My Notes:

References

Chapter 1

ASCL (Association of School and College Leaders) (2019) 'The Forgotten Third'. ascl.org.uk/Our-view/Campaigns/The-Forgotten-Third

Department for Education (2013) *National Curriculum in England: science programmes of study* (subject content for Biology, Chemistry, Physics). gov.uk/government/publications/national-curriculum-in-england-science-programmes-of-study

Department for Education (2013) *National Curriculum in England: English programmes of study* (subject content for English). gov.uk/government/publications/national-curriculum-in-england-english-programmes-of-study

Heathcote, Jo (2017) *AQA GCSE English Language for post-16: A one-year course.* London, Collins.

Heathcote, Jo, Davis, Caroline, Slater, Emma, Williams, Nicole (2020) *Reimagine Key Stage 3 English.* London, Collins.

Chapter 3

Batsleer, Janet, Davies, Tony, O'Rourke, Rebecca, Weedon, Chris (2003) *Rewriting English: Cultural Politics of Gender and Class* (New Accents). London, Routledge. taylorfrancis.com/books/mono/10.4324/9781315015873/rewriting-english-janet-batsleer-tony-davies-rebecca-rourke-chris weedon

Heathcote, Jo, Davis, Caroline, Slater, Emma, Williams, Nicole (2020) *Reimagine Key Stage 3 English.* London, Collins.

Heathcote, Jo, Al-Jamri, Ali, Benjamin-Lewis, Joanne, Bhavsar, Payal, Boothman, Djamila Gavin, Jamila, Gould, Mike, Skinner, Lindsay (2022) *Through Our Eyes: 24 Brilliant Texts to Enrich Your GCSE English Curriculum.* London, Collins.

Heathcote, Jo, Al-Jamri, Ali, Benjamin-Lewis, Joanne, Bhavsar, Payal, Boothman, Djamila Gavin, Jamila, Gould, Mike, Skinner, Lindsay (2021) *Who We Are: 24 Brilliant Texts to Enrich Your KS3 English Curriculum.* London, Collins.

Morby, Adam (2014) 'Changes to the English Literature GCSE: A Sociocultural Perspective', *FORUM*, 56:3, pp.499–512. https://journals.lwbooks.co.uk/forum/vol-56-issue-3/article-6150/

NATE (National Association of Teaching English) (2020) 'The Decline in Student Choice of A Level English', *Teaching English*, Issue 24, pp.24–28.

nate.org.uk/wp-content/uploads/2020/06/NATE-Post-16-position-paper.pdf

Stonewall (2003) '18 November 2003: Section 28 Bites the Dust'. stonewall.org.uk/our-work/campaigns/18-november-2003-section-28-bites-dust

Teach First (2020) 'Missing Pages: Increasing Racial Diversity in the Literature We Teach'. teachfirst.org.uk/reports/missing-pages

Chapter 4

[Author name to be added] (2022) 'What word is missing? Knowledge retrieval in English is _____ and it isn't all about quotations', *Learning From My Mistakes: an English teacher's blog.* [learningfrommymistakesenglish.blogspot. com/2023/02/what-word-is-missing-knowledge.html]

Heathcote, Jo, Davis, Caroline, Slater, Emma, Williams, Nicole (2020) *Reimagine Key Stage 3 English.* London, Collins.

Heathcote, Jo, Al-Jamri, Ali, Benjamin-Lewis, Joanne, Bhavsar, Payal, Boothman, Djamila Gavin, Jamila, Gould, Mike, Skinner, Lindsay (2021) *Who We Are: 24 Brilliant Texts to Enrich Your KS3 English Curriculum.* London, Collins.

Heathcote, Jo and Appleton, Hannah (2022) *Reimagine Key Stage 3 Shakespeare.* London, Collins.

Quigley, Adam (2018) *Closing the Vocabulary Gap.* London, Routledge.

Rosenshine, Barak (2012) 'Principles of Instruction: Research-Based Strategies That All Teachers Should Know', *American Educator*, pp.12–39. [teachertoolkit.co.uk/ wp-content/uploads/2018/10/Principles-of-Insruction-Rosenshine.pdf]

Chapter 5

AQA (2017) 'Preparing to Teach: GCSE English Language and English Literature'. aqa.org.uk/subjects/english/gcse/english-language-8700/planning-resources?f. Resource+type%7C6=Prepare+to+teach+meetings

AQA Mark Scheme for GCSE English Language (2021) Paper 1, Question 2

Heathcote, Jo (2017) *AQA GCSE English Language for post-16: A one-year course.* London, Collins.

Heathcote, Jo (2018) *AQA GCSE (9–1) English Language Exam Practice.* London, Collins.

Chapter 6

AQA Mark Scheme for GCSE English Language (2021) Paper 1, Question 2

Dedication

Thanks to the team at HarperCollins for believing in this project and bringing it to life; to Eleanor White for helping me conceptualise it over a cup of coffee; and, as always, to Brian, Lydia and Alex for their patience with me while I am writing.

However, thanks must also go to the brilliant students I have had the pleasure to teach and work with over the past thirty years, who have kept me on my toes, fed my imagination and allowed me to share so much of the subject I love.

Acknowledgments

We are grateful to the following for permission to reproduce copyright material:

Extracts from "Science programmes of study: key stage 4. National curriculum in England", Department for Education, December 2014, https://www.gov.uk/government/publications/national-curriculum-in-england-science-programmes-of-study, pp.7,11,14, © Crown copyright 2014. Open Government Licence v2.0; Extracts from "English programmes of study: key stage 3, National curriculum in England", Department for Education, September 2013, https://www.gov.uk/government/publications/national-curriculum-in-england-english-programmes-of-study, pp.4, © Crown copyright 2013. Open Government Licence; An extract from "English programmes of study: key stage 4, National curriculum in England, July 2014, https://www.gov.uk/government/publications/national-curriculum-in-england-english-programmes-of-study, p.5, © Crown copyright 2014; A table from "GCSE English language: GCSE subject content and assessment objectives", Department for Education, https://www.gov.uk/government/publications/gcse-english-language-and-gcse-english-literature-new-content, p.6, © Crown copyright 2013. Open Government Licence; A table from "GCSE English literature: subject content and assessment objectives", Department for Education, https://www.gov.uk/government/publications/gcse-english-language-and-gcse-english-literature-new-content", © Crown copyright 2013. Open Government Licence; Table 'UK exam boards' proportion of pre-1917 and post-1917 texts in the GCSE English Literature Syllabus, before and after the change is implemented' from "Changes to the English Literature GCSE: a sociocultural perspective" by Adam Morby, FORUM, Vol 56 (3), 2014 https://journals.lwbooks.co.uk/forum/vol-56-issue-3/article-6150/. Reproduced by kind permission of the author; An extract from "What word is missing? Knowledge retrieval in English is _____ and it isn't all about quotations" Learning from my mistakes: an English teacher's blog, by Chris Curtis, 26/02/23 https://learningfrommymistakesenglish.blogspot.com/2023/02/what-word-is-missing-knowledge.html. Reproduced with kind permission of the author; Table showing learning journey – assessment objectives and question stems – through English Lang GCSE papers from AQA. 2017. 'Preparing to Teach: GCSE English Language and English Literature' PowerPoint resource, https://www.aqa.org.uk. AQA material is reproduced by permission of AQA; Extract from "A historical overview of English assessment at age 16" by Barbara Bleiman, February 2023, published online https://www.englishandmedia.co.uk/blog/historical-overview-of-english-assessment-at-age-16, copyright © 2023. Reproduced by kind permission of the English and Media Centre; And a table showing simplified version, levels 1 to 4 mark scheme for GCSE English Language, Mark Scheme for GCSE English Language, Paper 1, Question 2 https://www.aqa.org.uk. AQA material is reproduced by permission of AQA.

In some instances we have been unable to trace the owners of copyright material, and we would appreciate any information that would enable us to do so.

Photographs

The publishers gratefully acknowledge the permission granted to reproduce the copyright material in this book. Every effort has been made to trace copyright holders and to obtain their permission for the use of copyright material. The publishers will gladly receive any information enabling them to rectify any error or omission at the first opportunity.

p.16 Jon Naustdalslid/Shutterstock, p.18 Monkey Business Images/Shutterstock, p.25 StunningArt/Shutterstock, p.36 Andrea Colarieti/Shutterstock, p.38 Carla Nichiata/Shutterstock, p.54 ESB Professional/Shutterstock, p.67 Ajdin Kamber/Shutterstock, p.67 Motortion Films/Shutterstock, p.70 Monkey Business Images/Shutterstock, p.83 Monkey Business Images/Shutterstock, p.90 fizkes/Shutterstock, p.95 Valery Sidelnykov/Shutterstock, p.98 wavebreakmedia/Shutterstock, p.101 keith morris/Alamy Stock Photo.